You Are Wonderfully MADE!

The Riverboat Adventures

1. *Escape Into the Night*
2. *Race for Freedom*
3. *Midnight Rescue*
4. *The Swindler's Treasure*
5. *Mysterious Signal*
6. *The Fiddler's Secret*

Adventures of the Northwoods

1. *The Disappearing Stranger*
2. *The Hidden Message*
3. *The Creeping Shadows*
4. *The Vanishing Footprints*
5. *Trouble at Wild River*
6. *The Mysterious Hideaway*
7. *Grandpa's Stolen Treasure*
8. *The Runaway Clown*
9. *Mystery of the Missing Map*
10. *Disaster on Windy Hill*

Let's-Talk-About-It Stories for Kids

1. *You're Worth More Than You Think!*
2. *Secrets of the Best Choice*
3. *You Are Wonderfully Made!*

LET'S TALK ABOUT IT
STORIES FOR Kids

You Are Wonderfully MADE!

LOIS WALFRID JOHNSON

BETHANY HOUSE PUBLISHERS
MINNEAPOLIS, MINNESOTA 55438

You Are Wonderfully Made!
Revised Edition 1999
Copyright © 1988, 1999
Lois Walfrid Johnson

Cover by the Lookout Design Group
Text illustrations by Jennifer Horton

The stories and characters in this book are fictitious. Any resemblance to actual persons, living or dead, is coincidental.

Published by Bethany House Publishers
A Ministry of Bethany Fellowship International
11400 Hampshire Avenue South
Minneapolis, Minnesota 55438
www.bethanyhouse.com

Printed in the United States of America by
Bethany Press International, Minneapolis, Minnesota 55438

Library of Congress Cataloging-in-Publication Data

CIP data applied for

ISBN 1–55661–654–6   CIP

To every kid
who has the courage to think and dream big
and follow in the footsteps
of
Jesus Christ

You are wonderfully made!

LOIS WALFRID JOHNSON is the bestselling author of more than twenty-five books. Her work has been translated into twelve languages and has received many awards, including the Gold Medallion, the C. S. Lewis Silver Medal, the Wisconsin State Historical Society Award, and five Silver Angels from Excellence in Media. Yet Lois believes that one of her greatest rewards is knowing that readers enjoy her books.

In her fun times Lois likes to camp, bike, cross-country ski, be with family and friends, and talk with young people like you. Lois and her husband, Roy, live in Minnesota.

Contents

Dear Parents

Dear Parents—

It has often been said that Christian values are better caught than taught. Perhaps this is most true in the area of sexuality. Day by day children sense your attitudes, your respect for the way God created you, and your belief in the sacredness of sex within marriage.

But concepts about sexuality should also be discussed. Your child needs correct information on which to build godly attitudes. Your conversations together will communicate that you value who you are as a sexual being and that your child's sexuality is a special gift.

You Are Wonderfully Made! was written to help you in those conversations. This book goes beyond information about human development to deal with attitudes and values from a Christian viewpoint. It presents situations that may be encountered by children in this age group or slightly older.

With other titles in this series, you probably read the stories together as you came to them. Because of the wide variation in children's maturity levels, you may want to read this book before sharing it with your son or daughter. You'll notice topics that you'll want to discuss if something comes up in their schooling. Or your child may have questions because of a TV program, conversations with friends, or events in your community. As you talk together, you'll have the opportunity to give your own input and shape your child's beliefs and values.

When you sense the time is right, do your best to find uninterrupted moments for talking together. As you read the stories, explain concepts in your own words. Take the stories in sequence over a period of time, or turn directly to a topic that relates to what is happening now. Or, if you like, plan a special overnight for talking through the book together.

If your child has questions he or she has not asked, reading these stories will encourage the freedom to do so. If you're not comfortable with some questions, be honest about your feelings. But then be willing to seek out answers. Your son or daughter will feel it's all right to express real concerns.

God bless you in the adventure of talking with your child about the beliefs and values you cherish. You, too, are wonderfully made!

To the Kids Who Read This Book

This book is about miracles.

"Miracles?" you ask.

That's right. Miracles about you.

"But miracles are something so big, so earthshaking that—"

That you never expect to be in on one?

"You got it. And isn't God the one in charge of miracles?"

Right again. God *is* the one in charge. But there's something you might need to think about. Miracles are all around you every day, even if you don't see them.

Take that honey sitting on your breakfast table.

This morning you put some of the sweet golden stuff on your toast and didn't give it a second thought. But did you know that to make one pound of honey, bees may travel 13,000 miles? That's crossing the United States from New York to California four times!

Or think about the only bird that can fly backward or hover like a helicopter in one spot. You guessed it—the hummingbird! When ruby-throated babies are just hatched, they're so small that one teaspoon holds four of them. Yet within three weeks those tiny hummingbirds are fully feathered and strong enough to leave the nest.

And what about those tulips growing outside your house? In the winter they seem dead and might be covered with snow. But every spring little green shoots push their way through the earth. Soon a bud appears, then a full-blown flower. What makes that tulip come back year after year? Why does it push its way up to grow into something beautiful for you?

Yet there are other, even bigger miracles. Each time you look in the mirror, you see one. Maybe you're thinking, *I don't even like the way I look. I sure don't feel like a miracle!* That's okay. You don't have to *feel* like one. Just the same, you *are*.

Do you know that your heart pumps five quarts of blood through your body in about sixty seconds? In just one year your heart pumps from 777,000 to over 1,600,000 gallons— enough to fill 97 to 200 railroad tank cars of 8,000 gallons each! When you think about that, do you suppose that maybe, just possibly, you're one of God's miracles?

This book will tell you about the miracle of how you came to be. It will help you understand the miracle of sex and why you're created the way you are. But this book also talks about more—your sexuality.

Sexuality has to do with how your being a boy or a girl affects your entire life. How do you feel about yourself because you're male or female? What attitudes do you have? How does the way you think about your sex affect your relationships?

Your sexuality involves your feelings, your mind, and your spirit, as well as your body. It involves your beliefs and your values. That's where choices come in.

Because your body is changing, you'll have new choices to face. That's part of growing up. Making choices can be fun, but also difficult, because you're deciding what side you want to be on. **The side you choose will make a difference in the kind of person you become.**

"But . . ." you say, "I don't *know* what side I want to be on."

The kids in this book often feel the same way. Like you, they have the opportunity to choose God's side, but another side wants to win. That's the side of sex you might read about. Or you might see it on TV or in movies and videos. That's the side you learn about from kids who don't love the Lord or know His plan for the way you're made.

God created sex to be something beautiful. That same big God created you in His own image—to be like *Him*!

As you read this book, you may find that you aren't quite ready for the information in a certain story. If so, that's okay. Go on to the next chapter. Later, when you face questions about a topic, go back to the story you missed.

Words that might not be familiar to you will be in *italics* the first time they're used. If you want help to pronounce those words or understand their meaning, check the list at the back of the book.

At the end of each story, you'll find questions. You may also have questions of your own. Talk about them with your mom or dad or another grown-up you trust. Think of ways to solve the problems the kids in the stories face. Think of ways to solve your own problems. Then turn the book upside down. Repeat the Bible verse to yourself until you receive the help it gives. Read the prayer or pray one of your own.

When you think about all that's changing in your life, it may seem a bit scary to you. You might wonder, "What if I make the wrong choice? What if I'm a big zero? What if kids make fun of me?"

If those thoughts come to you, remember those miracles you looked at and didn't see. The bees that travel 13,000 miles to make a pound of honey. The hummingbird smaller than a teaspoon. The tulip that pushed through the earth to become a flower for you. Your heart's ability to pump enough blood to fill 97 to 200 railroad tank cars in one year. **Then remember that the God of miracles, who created you as the person you are, has given you an even bigger miracle—His Son, Jesus.**

The Bible describes Jesus when He was twelve years old: "Jesus grew both in body and in wisdom, gaining favor with God and people" (Luke 2:52, TEV). Whatever you face, He's been there before you.

Think about the gigantic footprints a dinosaur or a huge monster would make. Yet the footprints Jesus made when He walked on this earth are even larger. Jesus left the biggest footprints of anyone who ever lived. His footprints are so gigantic that you can walk in them, no matter how big your feet. Your friends can walk in them, your sister, brother, mom, or dad. If everyone in the whole world chose to walk in the footprints of Jesus, they could—because that's what Jesus wants.

Remember? He said, "Follow me."

You may already have learned to ask the question, "What would Jesus do?" Take the next step. Pray, "Jesus, what do you want *me* to do?" Be honest with Him. Tell Him right up front, "I need your help." Then walk in the footprints Jesus has given you.

So are you ready to discover that you are wonderfully made? Are you ready to follow God, the Creator of miracles, and His Son, the Worker of miracles?

Come on! The adventure begins.

Carlee's
Questions

As water from the shower sprayed Carlee's back, she felt good all over. It was Saturday morning, and the day stretched out before her. *No homework!* she thought. As soon as she finished dusting a couple of rooms, she could do whatever she wanted.

Coming out of the shower, Carlee caught a glimpse of herself in the mirror. For a moment she stood there, looking at her body. *I'm changing*, she thought. Carlee liked what she saw and wondered how it would feel to be a woman.

She was still wondering as she dusted Mom's bedroom. There she discovered a new book. Dropping down on the floor, Carlee started turning the pages.

This is exactly what I want to know!

Just then Mom came in. "Oh good, you found the book I bought for you yesterday. Why don't you read it, and then we can talk, okay?"

Carlee went to her room and started right in. The first chapter was about how every living thing grows:

A helpless kitten becomes a cat able to hunt her

own food. A slender-legged fawn loses its spots and begins to look like its mother. A one-inch baby kangaroo, or joey, changes into a powerful traveler.

Human beings also grow. You changed from an infant into a toddler. You learned to talk and run and climb. You learned to study and use your mind. As you played with other children, you developed physically and emotionally.

You also discovered what it means to become responsible—to do those things your parents ask you to do. As they learned they could trust you, they began giving you more freedom. They let you try new things.

During all those changes, your *pituitary gland* regulated most of your growth. Located at the base of your brain, the pituitary is the master gland of your body.

When your body reaches the age of *puberty*, there's another change. The word *puberty* describes the time when a boy or girl becomes physically mature enough to reproduce life. That doesn't mean they're emotionally ready. It takes many more years for that.

At puberty your pituitary gland sends a message to *ovaries*, two almond-shaped organs in your lower *abdomen* (you probably call it *stomach*). The pituitary gland says, "Begin sending *hormones!*" These hormones, *estrogen* in girls and *testosterone* in boys, start the development of sexual changes. A boy begins noticing male traits. A girl begins noticing female traits.

For you, as a girl, these changes usually start at about ten or eleven years of age, although they may begin a year earlier or a couple of years later. Your breasts start to change their shape and, over a period of years, develop like those of a woman. You notice hair under your arms and in your *pubic* area. The hair on your legs may begin to change, and your hips start to round out.

All of this is normal. They're signs that something else is happening in your body.

Carlee stopped for a minute to study the diagram of a girl's body. Then she settled herself into a more comfortable position and continued reading.

In the lower part of your abdomen or belly, you have reproductive organs that were very small when you were born. Your two ovaries contain thousands of tiny *eggs*. These are female sex cells. These eggs are so small that you can't see them. But starting at puberty, one of them is released about every twenty-eight days. That release of an egg from the ovary is called *ovulation*.

Near each ovary are delicate *Fallopian tubes* that have tiny fringed ends to help sweep the egg into a tube. The Fallopian tubes provide a passageway for the egg to travel from the ovary into the inside of the *uterus*.

If a male sex cell, or *sperm*, meets the egg in the outer one third of the tube, the egg may be *fertilized*. This means that the genetic center of the sperm unites with the genetic center of the egg to create the beginning of a baby. This is called *conception*.

Over the next four days, the fertilized egg, now called an *embryo*, moves down and attaches itself to the wall of the uterus. The embryo grows and begins to form a baby.

The uterus is shaped like a pear. Because the uterus is hollow inside and made with a stretchy muscle, it expands to give a baby room to grow.

The small end of the uterus is called the *cervix*. This contains the opening between the uterus and the passageway called the *vagina*. When a baby is born, it passes out of the uterus, through the cervix, and down through the vagina.

The opening of the vagina lies between a girl's legs and is protected by four soft folds of skin. There is a pair of small folds next to the vagina and a pair of larger folds on the outside. These are called the *labia*, or "lips."

A girl also has two other openings—the *anus* for passing solid waste, and the *urethra*, through which urine passes. The vagina lies between them. The *clitoris* is a small sensitive organ located just above the urethra.

Carlee stretched. There were still more things she wondered about, but just then Mom came by. "How are you doing?" she asked.

"Pretty good," answered Carlee. "But I'm finding a lot of big words."

Mom smiled. "There *are* a lot of big words, but you can go back to them and read their meanings whenever you want. Do you know what amazes me? The really special way a girl is created. When you think about how everything works together so that a woman can have a baby, it's—"

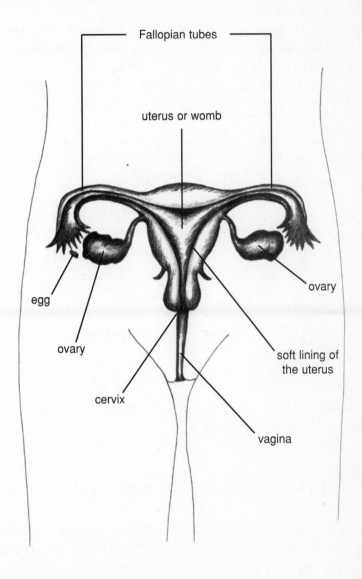

Fallopian tubes

uterus or womb

ovary

egg

ovary

soft lining of
the uterus

cervix

vagina

Female Reproductive Organs

"Awesome," Carlee said.

Mom nodded. "And miraculous!"

She dropped down in a chair. "There's something else you might wonder about. In the Bible, the uterus is called a *womb*. Let's read through the part that explains everything together. Then I can help you."

As Mom and Carlee talked, they matched the following words to the correct definitions:

____ 1. puberty
____ 2. ovaries
____ 3. Fallopian tubes
____ 4. vagina
____ 5. pituitary
____ 6. egg
____ 7. ovulation
____ 8. abdomen
____ 9. uterus, or womb
____ 10. hormone
____ 11. sperm

a. pear-shaped organ that holds a growing baby

b. master gland of the body

c. the time when an egg is released from the ovary, occurs about every twenty-eight days

d. the time when a boy or girl is physically able to reproduce life

e. female sex cell

f. female organs that have thousands of tiny eggs

g. male sex cell

h. passageways through which the egg travels on its way to the uterus

i. stomach

j. passageway a baby passes through to be born

k. starts the development of sexual traits in the body of a boy or girl

(Answers are on page 173.)

TO TALK ABOUT

▸ What questions would you like to ask your mom or dad or another adult you trust? They'll want to help you with anything you don't understand.

Know that the Lord is God. It is he who made us, and we are his; we are his people, the sheep of his pasture. Psalm 100:3

You're really awesome, God! Until now, I didn't know what a miracle worker you are. Thanks for all the things you've put together so that I can become a woman. Thanks for the fun of being a girl created by you. You're a big God!

Rob and Dad Talk

At first the flames of the campfire leaped high in the air. Then, as the logs burned down to embers, the boys began making s'mores.

As Rob put a roasted marshmallow and a piece of chocolate between graham crackers, he grinned. "Want some more, Dad?"

Dad grinned back and reached for the treat. Leaning against a log, he looked relaxed and happy. Rob felt the same way.

That weekend they were on a father-and-son camp-out. Rob felt glad for the time together. During the morning they canoed on the river. After lunch they swam in a quiet inlet near their campground. It had been a good day for both of them.

Before long, the dads and sons scattered to their own tents. The night air had started to cool down, and Rob crawled into his sleeping bag. Lying there, he decided this might be the time to ask the things he'd wondered about.

"Dad . . ." Rob's voice sounded uncertain.

By the light of the flashlight, Dad pushed his jacket and jeans into a corner. "What can I do for you?"

"Why do some kids my age have hair under their arms and others don't?"

"There's a lot of difference between boys," Dad answered. "As far as when they reach puberty, I mean."

"What's that?" asked Rob.

"Puberty? It's the time when a boy develops physically and is able to become a father or a girl develops physically and is able to become a mother. Girls usually reach that stage earlier than boys. A boy will probably enter puberty somewhere between twelve and fifteen years old, but it can be earlier or later."

Dad zipped open the window, and a dim light shone into the tent. Then he sat down on his sleeping bag. "Did you notice today how tall Larnell has grown? And he's already got lots of hair on his face. But Jack's the same age and a head shorter. He doesn't have *any* hair on his face."

Dad clicked off the flashlight and crawled into his sleeping bag. "And maybe you noticed something else when everyone showered after swimming. Some boys have hair around their penis or *scrotum* and others don't."

Rob had noticed all right and was afraid to say anything. "You know, I don't understand—" Rob stopped, feeling embarrassed. "I don't understand how everything works."

But Dad didn't sound embarrassed. "Do you mean how a boy's reproductive system works? It's really a miracle the way God created you."

For a moment Dad was quiet, as though thinking about where to begin. "Pretend we're at home and I have a diagram to show you, okay? You know that behind your penis and between your legs you have a small bag of skin. That's called the scrotum.

"Inside the scrotum you have two *testicles*. The testicles have a couple of jobs. They produce hormones called testosterone, which cause a boy to develop hair on his body at puberty—like the hair you noticed. Hormones also make a boy's voice get lower."

"Like Connor's voice, you mean? One minute it was high, then it was low. It kind of cracked."

"And he was embarrassed, wasn't he? But he didn't need to be. All of us fathers have had the same thing happen."

Dad went on. "The testicles also produce sperm, or male sex cells. Sperm are very small—smaller than the sharp end of a fish hook."

"What do they look like?"

"Under a microscope, sperm cells kind of look like tadpoles. Remember when we saw tadpoles swimming in shallow water? How they have little tails? Tails like that help sperm travel where they need to go.

"There's something else that's really interesting about the way you're created," Dad went on. "In order to survive, sperm need a temperature lower than your normal body temperature. So God put your testicles outside your body in the scrotum. Good idea, huh?"

In the dim light, Rob nodded.

"When a boy reaches puberty, his body begins to make a milky liquid in some glands near his penis. Sperm cells travel up a tiny tube called the *vas deferens* and mix with that liquid. The sperm and liquid together are called *semen*.

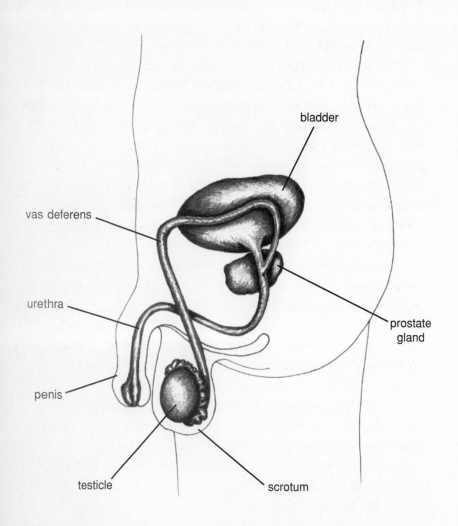

bladder

vas deferens

urethra

prostate
gland

penis

testicle

scrotum

Male Reproductive Organs

Then the semen goes out of the body through a small tube in the penis called the urethra."

"But that's where I go to the bathroom."

"You're right," Dad said. "Urine also leaves the body through that same tube in the penis. But urine and semen don't pass from the body at the same time."

A breeze had come up, and Dad closed the flap on the tent window. "There's something else you might wonder about," he said. "All males, even babies and little boys, have *erections*. That means their penis becomes firm and stands out from their body. Babies have erections even in their mother's womb. As a boy matures, he begins having more erections.

"He may also have what's called a *wet dream* or *nocturnal emission*. Sometimes as a boy dreams about a girl, his penis becomes erect and semen is released. If you wake up and wonder what's happened, your body is just getting rid of excess semen. It's a normal part of growing up. If your clothes are wet, get up and change them, then go back to sleep.

"Speaking of sleep—" Dad reached out and gave Rob's shoulder an affectionate shake. "But we had a good talk, didn't we? If you ever have any more questions—"

"Yup, I'll ask," Rob said as he pulled his sleeping bag up around his shoulders. It had been a really good day.

TO **TALK** ABOUT

▸ Rob felt good after he talked with his dad. Do you have more questions? Why don't you talk to your mom or dad or another adult you trust? They'll be glad you asked.

Match the following:

___ 1. puberty	a.	tube that carries urine and semen
___ 2. scrotum	b.	male sex cells
___ ___ 3. functions of testicles	c.	combination of sperm and milky liquid
___ 4. semen	d.	release of excess semen
___ 5. urethra	e.	produces sperm
___ 6. wet dream	f.	small bag of skin that holds testicles
___ 7. erection	g.	when a boy's penis becomes firm and stands out from his body
___ 8. sperm	h.	the time when a boy or girl becomes physically able to become a parent
___ 9. vas deferens	i.	produces hormones
	j.	tube that carries sperm to urethra

(Answers are on page 173.)

God saw all that he had made, and it was very good. Genesis 1:31a

Thank you, God, for the way you made me. All the special things you thought of are great! Help me to always respect what it means to be a boy created by you.

31

Saturday With Mom

When Carlee and Mom finished talking about how a girl's body is made, Carlee felt good about becoming a woman. Later on, she went back to the book Mom had given her. She'd heard girls talk about having a period and wanted to know more. Once again, she started reading:

You've already learned that about every twenty-eight days the ovary releases an egg cell. That egg passes through the Fallopian tube to the uterus.

The uterus, or womb, has a special lining prepared to nourish a baby. It contains many blood vessels that help a baby grow. If conception has not occurred, that lining, or tissue, isn't needed. It separates from the uterus. The tissue, along with the egg and waste blood, passes out through the vagina.

This process occurs about every twenty-eight days and is called *menstruation*. When girls menstruate they often say, "I'm having my period."

Girls usually have their first period somewhere

between the ages of nine and sixteen. Normally a period lasts from three to five days, but may be as long as seven. At first the periods may be irregular, with a girl skipping a month or two now and then. As time goes on, her cycle will probably become more regular. By marking a calendar, a girl can know about when her period will take place.

When Carlee finished reading, she had some questions. She was glad when Mom stopped in her room again. "How will I feel when I have a period?" Carlee asked.

"Sometimes girls have a little discomfort or crampy feeling in their abdomen, or they ache in their lower back. Usually this isn't serious. If you are uncomfortable, just tell me. But most girls keep on doing whatever they normally do."

"What do I do if I get my period?"

Mom went to the linen closet and brought back a box. "You can keep these *sanitary napkins* in a drawer so you have them if you start your period."

Mom opened the box. "These pads will protect your clothes and absorb the blood you pass. When you have your period, it's important to take a shower or bath and wash your *genital* area every day. It's also good to change pads fairly often—maybe four or five times a day."

"After you've used pads, you may want to try *tampons* instead. A tampon is a small roll of absorbent material you insert into your vagina. You can use both tampons and pads or either. You need to change a tampon when it becomes full of blood. Leaving tampons in for long periods of time—more than six hours—can lead to an illness called toxic shock syndrome. Although rare, it can be serious."

"What if I start having my period when I'm in school?" asked Carlee.

"Talk to a female teacher or go to the nurse's office. She'll help you," said Mom. "Once you start having periods, you can carry pads in your purse at the time of the month when you expect your period. Some school and public places have dispensers where you can buy pads or tampons."

"But they took the doors off the toilets."

Mom sighed. "I saw that the last time I visited your school. Why don't you ask the nurse if there's some place with more privacy? Or ask your gym teacher."

"What if kids know I have my period?"

"If you change your pad when needed, they won't know," Mom said. "You might feel like kids know, but they really won't unless you tell them. If you want, talk about it with Amber or another special girl friend. Maybe Amber will start having periods about the same time."

For a moment Mom was silent, as though thinking. "Do you know what would be fun? When you have your first period, why don't you and I do something special together? We'll celebrate this stage of your becoming a woman. Let's go out to eat or do something fun like that."

Carlee grinned. "Okay by me." For a moment she thought about all that would be happening to her body.

"You know, Mom—" Carlee stopped, then went on. "Sometimes I look forward to growing up, and sometimes I don't."

Mom leaned forward to hug Carlee. "I know. And it's okay

to feel that way. But that's something else God has done for you. When He created your body, He made it so you'll mature at your own pace.

"That may be different from when Amber or one of your other friends matures. Every girl is a little different. One girl will be first to start menstruating or wearing a bra. Another girl will be the last. Those changes come when your body is ready. Okay?"

Carlee nodded.

"Any more questions?"

Carlee smiled. "Not right now. But maybe tomorrow."

to **TALK** about

‣ What happens in a girl's body in order for her to have a period?

‣ What's the best way to keep track of when your period will be?

‣ Some kids talk about sex or the questions they have with just anybody. Why is it easy to pick up wrong information that way?

‣ Because kids mature at different rates, they may ask questions about sex at different ages. Your mom or dad may have talked with you before your friends have talked with their parents. Why is it important that you let those kids talk with their parents first?

▸ What questions do you have that you'd like to ask your mom or dad or another special person you trust?

And my God will meet all your needs according to his glorious riches in Christ Jesus. Philippians 4:19

Thank you, Creator God, for all the great things you did to make me the way I am. Help me when I get upset because my body changes faster or slower than other girls. Thanks that I don't have to worry about that. Thanks for being the one in charge!

More Than One Miracle

It was two o'clock in the morning when Joel felt Mom's hand on his shoulder. Through the fog of sleep, he heard her voice.

"Taffy's having her puppies. Want to see them being born?"

Joel had been waiting for this. Still rubbing the sleep out of his eyes, he stumbled out of bed and headed for a room off the kitchen.

His family had two Labradors—a black male named Fudge and a yellow female called Taffy. Now Taffy lay on a blanket in one corner. As she turned her head, her large brown eyes looked at Joel.

Dad had set up a large piece of cardboard, blocking off a part of the room. "Taffy knows you. She's so gentle I don't think she'll mind if you watch. But stay behind this cardboard so you don't upset her."

One puppy had already been born. As Joel watched, Taffy licked the little body. With its eyes still closed, the puppy was small and helpless.

"Can it see?" Joel asked.

Dad shook his head. "A puppy is blind when it's born. It'll open its eyes in about ten days or so."

A few minutes later a second puppy was born. It had a soft clear bag around it. As Joel watched, Taffy broke the bag with her teeth and freed the puppy. Again Taffy licked the little body, washing it off.

By now the first puppy had snuggled up to Taffy's stomach and started drinking milk. Joel pulled up a chair and watched every move. One by one, four more puppies were born. Each one seemed a miracle.

At last Joel crawled back into bed, but the next morning he had more questions. As Mom fixed breakfast, Joel found Dad in the family room. "How come Taffy's puppies are different colors?" he asked. "I thought they'd all look like her."

"That's because Fudge is their father," Dad said. "Because he's a black Lab, there are some black and some chocolate puppies. Only one was yellow, wasn't it? Because Fudge has dark hair, it shows up in his puppies."

"What do you mean?"

"Sometimes with animals we aren't sure who the father is. In our case we know it's Fudge. Because he's our dog, he stays here. But usually animals don't have a family the way human beings do."

"Like ours?"

"Like ours," Dad said. "Babies need a mother and a father to take care of them. That's why it's important that a mom and dad are married and committed to each other before they have children. Do you know what I mean by commitment?"

Joel thought for a moment. "That you love each other?"

"Right. Love is important. But commitment also means that your mom and I have promised to help each other. We've promised to be loyal to each other, to stay married and be together even if it's hard. Sometimes a mom or dad dies. Or they're separated by divorce. Those times are really difficult for a family. But even though a mom and dad are separated by divorce, they still love their children.

"Because God wanted children born within marriage, He made us in such a way that it takes both a mom and a dad to have a baby. Do you understand how a baby is created?"

"Not all of it," Joel said.

"Okay, you know how a boy's body is different from a girl's body. One of God's miracles is that those differences are just what is needed in order to create a baby. The Bible says that when a man and a woman are married, they become one flesh.

"A husband and wife like to have special alone times. That's a way of showing their love for each other. Because they're married and committed to each other, those times can be very beautiful.

"During those alone times, they may have what we call *sexual intercourse*. A man's penis becomes firm (an erection) and fits into a woman's vagina. The male sex cells called sperm are released from the man's body. Those sperm travel up the uterus into a woman's Fallopian tubes. If an egg has been released from one of the woman's ovaries, the egg and sperm meet.

"Only one sperm unites with an egg cell. When that happens, the egg has been fertilized. We say that conception has taken place. God has started a new life.

"The fertilized egg, or embryo, begins to divide and the cells multiply. One cell becomes two, two become four, until there are more and more cells. The embryo moves through the Fallopian tube and attaches itself to the wall of the uterus. If everything goes well, the cells keep multiplying. Slowly the new baby develops."

"Last night, what was the little bag around Taffy's puppies when they were born?" asked Joel.

"For a human baby it's called an *amniotic sac*, or bag of waters. The amniotic sac is a bag full of liquid called amniotic fluid. That fluid protects the baby from bumps and keeps it the right temperature. The *placenta* is an organ attached to the uterus, and it's full of blood vessels. Food and oxygen from the mother flow through the blood vessels of the placenta and through the *umbilical cord* to the baby."

"The what?"

"The umbilical cord. You know how you have a navel? You call it a belly button. Your cord stretched from there to the placenta. That's how you received food and oxygen before you were born. And your waste materials passed through the cord to the placenta."

"How long does it take?"

"For a baby to develop? For human babies about nine months. I remember how much fun it was to know that you were growing."

"So do I!" Mom said as she came into the room. "About thirteen weeks after conception, your body was completely formed. Yet you were only about three and a half inches long."

"We saw you on *ultrasound* and took pictures," Dad said. "We carried those pictures around for months. We showed you off to all our friends!"

Joel grinned.

"One day when the doctor was checking your mom, I got to hear your heartbeat. Then as you got bigger, I often put my hand on your mom's abdomen and felt you kick."

Joel laughed.

"Your mom kept getting bigger and bigger until finally you were ready to be born. When that time comes, the muscles in a woman's uterus begin to squeeze and push the baby down into the vagina. The bag of waters breaks, and the vagina stretches to let the baby pass through."

Dad's eyes lit with excitement. "The most special moment of all was when I watched your birth."

"You got to see me being born?"

Dad nodded. "I was right there with your mom. The minute you were born, the doctor held you up and said, 'It's a boy!' You let out a big squall, and it was the most wonderful cry in the world. I thought, 'Wow! Thank you, Lord! He sounds healthy!' "

"Some fathers even get to cut the umbilical cord," Mom said.

"Doesn't that hurt the baby?"

"Nope. It's like cutting hair or fingernails," Dad said.

"They wrapped you in a blanket and put you in my arms." Mom's face glowed, just thinking about it. "All I could say was, 'You're beautiful!' I loved you so much that I started to cry."

Inside, Joel felt warm with that love. Then suddenly he

thought of his friend Matt. "What about kids who are adopted?"

"The birth process is just the same," Dad said. "It's just that for some reason—maybe many reasons—the mother isn't able to take care of her baby. She allows a mom and dad who want a baby very much to become parents. Are you thinking of Matt?"

Joel nodded.

"The first time his mom and dad saw him was just as exciting for them as when we first saw you. His mom cried even harder than your mom. And Matt's parents love him the way we love you."

"Any more questions?" asked Dad.

"Nope!" said Joel. Jumping up, he went out into the kitchen. Taffy's puppies were snuggled up against her, and Joel sat down to watch.

TO TALK ABOUT

▸ This story talked about two different miracles for Joel. What were they?

▸ Have you ever seen a puppy or kitten being born? Or, if you live on a farm or ranch, have you seen calves, lambs, or other animals being born? What do you remember about those special times?

▸ Animals love and protect their new babies. How does your family protect and care for you?

▸ How did God make a special plan for creation so that children are born in families?

▶ What does the word *conception* mean?

▶ In what ways does God's miracle of birth seem especially wonderful to you?

For this reason a man will leave his father and mother and be united to his wife, and they will become one flesh. Gen-esis 2:24

I'm beginning to see how great you are, God! Thanks that in order to be born, I needed both a mom and a dad. Thanks for making me one of your BIG miracles!

I Wonder....

Later on, Carlee, Rob, and Joel had more questions. Here's what they discovered:

What About Twins?

Twins develop in one of two ways. Sometimes a fertilized egg or embryo divides completely in two, and two separate embryos or babies develop. In that case, *identical twins* are born. They will be the same sex and look alike.

Other times two sperm cells fertilize two eggs. Then *fraternal twins* are born. They can be the same sex, or one might be a boy and the other a girl. They may be as different as two children in the same family, even though they're born at the same birth.

Why Am I a Girl? Or a Boy?

It has to do with a little threadlike particle called a *chromosome*. When conception takes place, an egg has twenty-three chromosomes and the sperm has twenty-three. There are two kinds of sperm. One is called an X chromosome sperm. When that unites with an egg, a girl is born. The other is called a Y chromosome sperm. When that unites with an egg, a boy is born. Eggs always have X chromosomes.

What Does It Mean When the Bible Talks About Circumcision?

A boy is born with a loose fold of skin over the end of his penis. *Circumcision* is a simple operation that removes the skin and makes it easier to keep the penis clean.

In Bible times God told Abraham and his descendants to circumcise their male children. It was a sign that God and His people had a special relationship. The Bible tells us that after Jesus was born, Mary and Joseph took Him to the Temple to be circumcised when He was eight days old.

At the present time, some boys are circumcised and others aren't. If parents want their son circumcised, a doctor takes care of it soon after a baby's birth.

What Is Acne?

The word *acne* refers to pimples and blackheads, a problem you may call *zits*. Having acne isn't much fun, but it's a common experience for both boys and girls in the years during puberty and sometimes after.

Avoid picking or squeezing pimples. They may become infected and leave scars. Because your skin may be more oily then it used to be, cleanse it carefully. If you continue to have a problem, ask your mom or dad whether you need to see a skin doctor.

New Hope for Heidi

Heidi took the stairs two at a time and headed straight for her bedroom. Slamming the door behind her, she threw herself down on the bed.

Tears pressed against her eyes as she relived that awful moment at school. Two boys had bumped into her—purposely, it seemed.

They'd exclaimed, *"Oh, excu-u-u-se me!"* Then they'd called her that awful name. Not even to herself would Heidi repeat it. It hurt too much.

Biting her lip, Heidi had kept the tears back, thinking, *Not for anything am I gonna let those creeps know how I feel!*

But now she wondered, *Why, God? Why did I have to develop earlier than the other girls?* For a long time she'd been wearing baggy sweat shirts to hide her growing chest. It didn't work anymore. Just then Heidi heard a knock on the bedroom door. Jumping up, she opened it. Her seventeen-year-old sister, Cher, popped in. "Wanna go get Mom's birthday present? Dad said I could take the car."

Heidi liked going places with Cher. Fifteen minutes later the two of them walked into the mall.

After looking in two stores, Cher said, "Let's try that little place where we went last time. Remember where it is? I can't think of its name."

As they headed into the large open area at the center of the mall, Heidi suddenly stopped. "Let's go somewhere else instead."

"How come?"

"See those boys? They're from school."

Heidi started off in another direction, and Cher followed. "Why are you running away from them?"

Heidi kept walking.

But Cher didn't give up. "How come?"

Still Heidi didn't answer. She felt like crying again, just remembering what had happened.

"Hey, c'mon, I'm your big sis. You can tell me. Let's duck in here, and I'll treat you to a soda."

And so the story came out. Cher listened without talking until Heidi finished. Then she said, "It's just hormones."

"It's what?"

"Hormones. They cause sexual traits to develop—male traits in boys and female traits in girls. That's why your hips are changing, too. Pretty soon my jeans will fit you."

"But no one else—" Heidi broke off. "I mean—"

Cher's voice was soft. "It's not up to you when your hormones kick in. You can't control it. That's why one girl matures faster than another. And that's okay. For one girl, it's early. For another, it's late. Either way, it's just normal."

"But I feel so stupid!"

"You shouldn't. One way isn't right and the other way wrong. It's only what kids make it—especially boys who aren't very smart."

"But it's so *awful* when they tease me!"

"You're right, it is. When I was your age, they called me the very same thing."

"They did? What did you do?"

"I cried. I hunched my shoulders, hoping kids wouldn't see. I kept making excuses to not go to school. Finally Mom caught on to what was wrong. She told me all that stuff about my body being a gift from God. I didn't believe her. In fact, I got so mad at one boy that I hauled off and gave him a bloody nose."

Heidi giggled. She thought about the boys who teased her and imagined blood dripping from each nostril. "That's what I should do!"

But Cher shook her head. "It didn't help. Besides, you'd get in big trouble with your teachers. The next day the guy brought back his buddies. *All* of them started calling me names. And managed to stay far enough away—"

"So you couldn't slug 'em." Again Heidi giggled. "What scaredy cats!"

Cher grinned.

"Then what happened?"

"It took a while, but I finally got smart. I decided, 'They're having all that fun teasing me. I'm not gonna give 'em the satisfaction.' I considered the source and didn't let 'em get to me."

"But how did you ever do that?"

Now Cher's eyes were serious. "Kids who are unhappy

on the inside want to make others unhappy. If they can't get through to you, they'll go on to someone else. It's no fun teasing someone who doesn't cry or get mad."

Heidi finished her soda, and they stood up. "But . . ." She still had more questions.

"I mean it." Cher grinned. "It usually works. And someday the boys will grow up."

As they started toward the center of the mall, Cher gave her a quick hug. "Pretty soon you'll be as cute as I am."

This time it was Heidi's turn to smile. She would like that.

TO **TALK** ABOUT

‣ What causes some girls to develop before others?

‣ Is there a right or a wrong time as to when a girl's body changes? Why or why not?

‣ When kids tease others about their appearance, what does it show about the kid who does the teasing?

‣ Both boys and girls often experience teasing about the way they look. (Your ears, your nose, the hair on your arms, or whatever.) In what ways have you learned to handle teasing? Did the kids stop teasing you, or did you learn to live with it? Give an example.

‣ Do you have people with whom you can talk if someone keeps picking on you in a really mean way? Who are those people? Don't be afraid to tell them what is happening.

‣ Why can learning how to live with something difficult seem like a miracle?

‣ What do you believe your Creator God thinks about the way He made your body? Why do you believe that?

‣ How did people make fun of Jesus? For some big clues, see Matthew 15:1; Matthew 16:1; and Luke 22:63–64. When kids tease you, how can you follow in the footsteps of Jesus?

May those who are wise understand what is written here, and may they take it to heart. The Lord's ways are right, and righteous people live by following them, but sinners stumble and fall because they ignore them. Hosea 14:9 (TEV)

Jesus, you know that it's not fun being different. You have been the most different person on earth for my sake! But help me know how to handle teasing. Thanks for loving me just the way I am.

French Fries
and Love

Book in hand, Jill flopped down on her bed and rolled onto her stomach. Mom had said she could bring her friend Kim home from school. It had been fun having time together.

Now Kim leaned forward. "Is that your sister's book about dating?"

Jill flipped pages. "Yup. Here's where we left off." She began reading aloud. " 'Love isn't something that just happens. You choose whom you love or don't love.' "

Kim stopped her. "Just a minute. What does that mean?"

"Let me finish," Jill said and kept on reading. " 'Some people say, "I fell in love. I just couldn't help myself." But—' "

Again Kim interrupted. "That's true. I *do* fall in love. If I like a boy, I like him. And right now I like Dusty. What's so bad about that?"

"What's *good* about it?" Jill's blue eyes met Kim's brown ones. Jill had never liked Dusty because of the way he acted. More than once the two girls had talked about how he treated others.

Jill went back to the book. " 'Some people say, "I fell in

love. I just couldn't help myself." But early in every relationship there's a moment of choice, whether we think about it or not. We decide, "I'm not interested in that boy as more than just a friend." Or we tell ourselves, "I like that boy. I hope he becomes my special friend." ' "

"That's true," Kim said. "I decide, all right. When I meet a boy, I know real soon if he's the one for me. I don't know why my mom won't let me start dating."

Jill sighed. "Kim, you're missing the whole point of the book. We can know a lot of people and be nice to them. But the book says there are times when we should choose to *not* become special friends with someone—especially someone we feel romantic about. We can wind up getting hurt."

"Oh, phooey!" Kim said. "You choose your friends, and I'll choose mine." Then she grinned. "Of course, you can keep choosing *me*!"

Jill rolled off the bed and stood up. "C'mon. Mom left money and said we could bike to McDonald's. She won't be home for a while."

A short time later, the girls slid into a booth. As Kim picked up her first French fry, she glanced out the window. "Look! Dusty and Chris!"

Jill felt glad to see Chris. As she and Kim watched, the two boys bought hamburgers, then headed over to sit with the girls.

Moments later, Dusty tugged a strand of Kim's long brown hair. "Hey, kid, how you doing?" Pushing his baseball cap to a cocky angle, he smiled lazily. "Did you see me at the game Saturday? Got the best hit of the whole team."

Kim nodded, her eyes shining. "You were a big hero!"

"Well, next game I'll do even better. Just keep your eyes on ol' Dusty."

Chris coughed and winked at Jill, as though guessing how she felt about Dusty's bragging.

Jill smiled back at Chris. "You got a hit that brought in two runs," she told him. But instead of bragging about it, Chris just nodded and grinned.

As the four of them ate, Jill started thinking. *That's what the book was talking about! I can choose to like Chris or choose to like Dusty. And I like more things about Chris than about Dusty. A whole lot more!*

Soon the boys finished eating and started to leave. Chris turned back. "See you at the church car wash, Jill."

Jill waved, then watched as Chris crossed a large open area. Ahead of him, Dusty and a young mother reached the double doors at the same time. With her right arm she held a baby. Her left hand clung to a young boy.

While the mother leaned into one door to push it open, Dusty hurried through the other. Following Dusty, the little boy strained ahead. Caught off balance, the mother almost fell.

In the next instant, the door swung back, catching the boy in the face. His yowl filled the store.

Jill jumped up. "Oh! Did you see that?" She rushed forward to help, but Chris was there ahead of her.

"Can I help you?" he asked the mother.

"Please." She looked grateful.

Chris led the boy to one side, away from the door and out of the traffic. Still holding the baby, the mother knelt down beside her son to comfort him.

Before long, the boy stopped crying and smiled up at Chris. As Jill watched, Chris helped the mother and children to their car.

Jill went back and sat down with Kim. "Watch out for number one, that's Dusty!"

"Are you kidding?" Kim asked. "It was an accident. Dusty didn't mean for the little boy to get hurt."

"Dusty was the *cause* of him getting hurt! And the mom almost fell! Did you see Dusty push ahead? He's the rudest person I know!"

"You're just jealous because he didn't pay attention to you."

"Are you serious?" Jill's anger felt like lava pouring out of a volcano.

But Kim's thoughts had already raced on. "Isn't he just the very best?"

"Who?"

"Dusty, of course! Who else?"

Jill groaned. "Kim, does Dusty ever think about anyone besides himself?"

As though the question had never occurred to her, Kim stared at Jill.

"Does Dusty ever go to church?"

Kim thought for a moment. "No, I guess not. What does that have to do with it?"

"You know that book we were reading? It talked about choosing Christians for our best friends."

"What's the big deal? I'm not going to *marry* Dusty. I just *like* him. When I get old enough, maybe he'll ask me out."

"If you start going with a guy like Dusty, you'll keep going

FRENCH FRIES AND LOVE

out with guys just like him. And Dusty thinks of only one person—himself."

"But he's fun, too." Kim sighed. "And he's really romantic! When I'm ready to get married, I'll find someone who goes to church."

Jill didn't believe her but knew she couldn't change Kim's mind. As Jill gathered up her food wrappers and tray, she thought ahead to the next afternoon. *I can hardly wait to see Chris again. It's fun just being in a group together.*

TO TALK ABOUT

‣ From what you know about Chris and Dusty, which boy do you respect the most? Why?

‣ Which boy do you think would be most thoughtful of the girl he someday marries? Why?

‣ Which girl, Jill or Kim, do you respect the most? Why?

‣ Jesus can use our friendships as an opportunity for us to tell others about Him. Yet some kids think, "I'll go out with that boy—or that girl—and I'll witness so that kid becomes a Christian." Do you think it actually works that way? Why or why not?

‣ Why is it important to spend a lot of time with *groups* of friends instead of getting involved with one person? If you're a boy, what are things you can learn in that way? If you're a girl, what can you learn?

‣ **When you choose Christians for your best friends, you meet other kids through them. Soon**

you know a whole group of Christian kids who are fun to be with. Why is that important?

▸ Kim described Dusty as being "really romantic." What is your idea of "romantic"?

▸ Does the word "romantic" describe someone who is faithful and true to his friends? Why or why not? Give reasons for your answer.

▸ **A person who is really a friend won't ask you to do something that hurts you.** What does it mean to have friends who choose the best for you? Think of an example.

▸ If you choose Christians as your special friends, does it *always* mean you won't have any problems? Why or why not? What are some things you should look for, even when you're with Christian kids? How can *you* help other kids be strong?

Do not be yoked together with unbelievers. For what do righteousness and wickedness have in common? Or what fellowship can light have with darkness? 2 Corinthians 6:14

Jesus, please give me special friends who are Christians—friends who will help me be strong. But, Lord, I also want to help them be strong in you. If you want me to get married someday, I want to marry a Christian who loves you the way I do. In your name, Jesus, I ask you for exactly the right person at the right time. Thank you!

Jason's Choice

Jason jumped down from the school bus and turned around. Sure enough, Tanya was looking through the window. Jason waved good-bye to her.

Tanya waved back. Even through the glass, her smile lit up her soft brown eyes. *She is the greatest!* Jason thought for the hundredth time.

As he headed down the block, Kent and Del fell into step beside him. "Wanna come over for a while?" Kent asked.

Jason remembered Dad's words. *"I don't want you hanging out with those kids."*

But when Dad didn't know, Jason did it anyway. He liked Kent and Del. Sure, sometimes they wanted him to do things he shouldn't. *But I can handle it,* Jason thought.

Aloud he said, "Yeah, I'll stop for a while." He knew why they were going to Kent's house. His mom and dad would both be working. No one would be home.

While they were shooting baskets, Del and Kent started

talking about the girls at school. As they talked about one girl, then another, the jokes got worse. Jason felt uncomfortable.

But what can I do? he wondered. *If I say anything, they'll laugh at me, too.*

Then Kent started talking about Tanya.

"That's not true!" Jason's words exploded.

"Hey, what's with you?" Kent asked as he tossed the ball to Del.

"She's not like you said! Quit talking about her!"

Instead, Kent started a singsong chant. "Jason loves Tanya! Jason loves Tanya!"

Del joined in. "Tanya loves Jason!"

"Aw, forget it!" Jason exclaimed.

Kent threw down the basketball. "C'mon, I wanna show you something."

Jason and Del followed Kent into the garage. Stacked along one wall were newspapers and magazines for a paper drive. Kent dug down into a different pile and pulled out a bunch of magazines.

"Take a look at these, you guys," he said. "I found some of my old man's magazines."

Kent tossed a magazine his way and Jason caught it. It took only a glance at one page and Jason felt sick all the way through. As though the magazine burned him, Jason threw it down.

"No wonder you guys have such dirty minds! I have to get home."

"Who you trying to kid?" Kent asked him. "You don't

have to go for another hour yet. What's the matter with you? No one will catch us reading."

Just then a picture of Tanya's face, smiling through the bus window, flashed through Jason's mind. He started out of the garage.

"Hey, what are you, religious or something?" Kent jeered.

Del joined the teasing. "You're a Jesus freak!"

"I don't want to read that junk," Jason called back.

"Aw, c'mon," Kent said. "You'll like the pictures."

Their jeers followed Jason as he started down the street. For a moment he slowed down, knowing they wouldn't forget this. *Next time I see 'em they'll be mad. Maybe they won't be my friends anymore.* Thinking about that, Jason stopped.

Standing on the sidewalk, he looked back. It took only a moment to decide. "I don't want to think that way about girls."

Jason started out again, then remembered. "Tomorrow I'll see Tanya again."

The rest of the way home he didn't look back once.

TO **TALK** ABOUT

▶ What kind of magazines were in Kent's garage?

▶ The word *pornography* refers to writing and pictures that make sex dirty. How had reading pornographic magazines affected Kent and Del?

▶ If someone spends a lot of time thinking sinful

thoughts, how will it affect the way he or she acts? If someone thinks about good things, how will it affect the way that person acts? See Psalm 119:11 and 2 Timothy 2:22 for clues.

▶ Why did Jason refuse to look at the magazines? Why will that help him keep a better attitude toward girls?

▶ Jason had to choose whether he wanted to be one of the guys or do what he felt was right. He made a good choice, even though it brought teasing from his friends. When have you needed to make a difficult choice? How did you feel about yourself after you made a good choice?

▶ **If you have a problem with thinking thoughts that you know are sinful, ask Jesus to forgive you. Then ask Him to make your mind clean. Next put good thoughts into your mind. The best way to do that is to memorize Bible verses.** When a wrong thought edges into your mind, refuse to think about it. Instead, repeat a Bible verse right away. Keep repeating that verse for as long as needed.

▶ A good verse might be Philippians 4:8. What are some other verses that could help you? Copy them onto note cards so you can repeat them to yourself and remember them.

▶ If you have trouble with your thought life, talk with a responsible grown-up who can help you. It also helps to get regular exercise and do things that take your mind off negative or sinful ideas. What are some fun things you can do with kids who care about thinking good thoughts? Are there activities in which you can take part? Name some of them.

May my spoken words and unspoken thoughts be pleasing even to you, O Lord my Rock and my Redeemer. Psalm 19:14 (TLB)

Jesus, I want to have clean words and clean thoughts. Help me to store your words in my heart so they keep me from sinning. Thank you, Jesus, for walking in holy ways. I choose to follow in your big footsteps.

Are Boys Really Better?

Gerry slid onto the tractor seat. It felt good to curl her fingers around the large steering wheel. When she first started driving the tractor, she'd been afraid of it. Now it had become her friend.

What a great day! she thought. Haying was fun on mornings like this. From a cloudless sky, the sun beat down on the road stretching out before her. If the weather held, they'd get everything in before rain edged over the horizon.

For a moment the breeze lifted Gerry's hair, tossing it in her face. As she pulled the long strands out of her eyes, she wished she'd brushed her hair into a ponytail. Shifting the tractor into gear, she took a quick look at the hay wagon behind her.

"Either sit down or hang on!" she called.

Her two younger cousins waved, and each slung an arm around the posts at the front of the wagon. Todd and Kenny were there for the summer. Gerry had to admit she was getting mighty tired of their company.

Why does Dad keep asking them back every June? she

wondered. *They're almost my age, yet they don't do nearly the work.*

As Gerry drove onto the gravel road, stones kicked up around the tractor. A trail of dust billowed behind the wagon.

When she headed into a field, Dad was already there, using the baler. Gerry watched as one bale after another shot up and then back, falling into the nearly full wagon behind Dad's tractor.

Once again Gerry twisted around to check on her cousins. By now they were wrestling. Todd had Kenny pinned dangerously close to the edge of the wagon.

"Hey, you guys, quit it!" shouted Gerry. "If I start up suddenly, you'll fall off."

Facing forward again, she saw Dad motion to her. "Get a move on!" his arms seemed to say.

Gerry pulled up behind Dad's baler. "What took you so long?" he asked.

Without waiting for an answer, Dad hopped down to unhitch Gerry's wagon. She set the brake and went to help, but Dad was still impatient. "You should have been a boy," he grumbled. "You never work the way a boy would."

Hot tears welled up in Gerry's eyes. More than once she had told her dad, *"I can't help the way I was born."* Instead of trying again, she leaned down, hiding her face as she hooked the chains under the hitch.

All day long, Gerry drove between the field and barn, but her thoughts were elsewhere. Like a video, one memory after another appeared before her eyes.

Mom telling her, *"We didn't have a girl's name picked*

out for you. You were going to be Gerald instead of Ger-
aldine."

A neighbor saying, *"When you were only three years
old, you wanted to do boys' work. One day I saw you trying to carry large stones for your dad."*

By midafternoon Gerry was tired of thinking about the
way things were. *I've tried and tried. But does it do any
good? Does Dad love me at all? I just want to please him.*

That day, for the first time all summer, they finished
work early. Mom had a good supper fixed. As everyone dug
into the roast beef and potatoes, Dad looked at Todd and
Kenny. "Want to go for a swim when we're done eating?"

"Sure thing!" they exclaimed and started eating faster.

Watching them, Gerry thought about how good it would
feel to dive into the cool water. She imagined the water clos-
ing over her warm, dusty body and the pull of her muscles
in a long swim.

Left out again! she thought. *It would be fun being with
Dad. Maybe just once . . .*

"Can I go, too?" Gerry asked him.

Dad shook his head. "This is only for boys."

Like the rush of water ready to spill over a dam, Gerry
felt anger and despair rise within her. She wanted to cry out,
"I'm worth something, Dad! I'm worth something, even
though I'm a girl!"

But she had said those things before, and it hadn't
helped.

Without a word Gerry stood up and carried her dishes to
the sink. As she set them down, she turned and looked back

at Dad, still sitting at the table. *I'm gonna try once more!* she decided.

Soon Mom finished her coffee and went to find the boys' swimsuits. Todd and Kenny left to change clothes, and Gerry sat down across the table from Dad.

"I want to tell you something," she said, facing Dad squarely. "I want to tell you how I feel."

Dad looked at Gerry, as though surprised at her tone of voice.

A nervous feeling started in Gerry's stomach, but she kept on. "All my life you've wanted me to be something I can't be. I'm not a boy. I'm a girl! I can't help that. But you make me feel like I'm no good!"

Dad stared at Gerry as though not believing what he heard. For the first time in her life, Gerry stared back instead of looking at the floor.

Dad was the first to look away. As he set down his coffee cup, his hand shook and the cup rattled in the saucer.

For a long moment, Dad sat there without speaking, his head bowed. When he finally spoke, his voice sounded strange and far away. "I'm sorry, Gerry," he said, still looking down. "That's what my ma and pa always told me. No matter what I did, they'd say, 'You're no good. You're no good.' "

Dad's broad shoulders began to shake, and Gerry felt scared. She'd never seen Dad cry before. When he looked up, there were tears in his eyes.

"I heard it so often, I always thought I was no good. I've passed that feeling on to you."

Gerry searched his eyes, wondering what to say. The pain in Dad's face was like the pain she'd felt all these years.

Dad spoke again. "I'm sorry, Gerry. I'm very sorry."

In the quiet room, Gerry heard the ticking of the clock. The moment seemed to stretch out forever. But at last Gerry knew what to do.

Standing up, she slowly circled the table. For the first time since she was a little girl, she gave her dad a hug.

TO **TALK** ABOUT

▸ What clues tell you that Gerry's dad valued boys more than girls?

▸ Because of the way he treated her, how did Gerry feel about being a girl? How do you think God feels about her being a girl?

▸ Why did it take courage for Gerry to tell her dad what was wrong?

▸ When Gerry's dad talked about feeling no good, he said, "I've passed that feeling on to you." What does it mean to pass a feeling on to someone else?

▸ Do you think Gerry's dad will change the way he treats her? Why or why not?

▸ If her dad *doesn't* change, what kind of people could Gerry talk with for encouragement? Why is it important that Gerry knows she's valuable exactly the way she is?

▸ **Sometimes it's not possible to change the way other people treat us. Yet if we ask God, He can help us change the way we feel about what is happening to us.** Are there ways in which you hurt because of the way people have treated you? You can talk with an adult you trust about it. That person can pray with you and ask God to show you good things about yourself.

▸ In God's sight is your being a boy or a girl ever an accident? How do you know?

For you created my inmost being; you knit me together in my mother's womb. Psalm 139:13

Father God, thank you for creating me just the way I am. Thank you that you're the one who decided whether I'm a boy or a girl. Help me value the person I am now and the person I will become as I grow older. Give me the healing I need.

74

All My Problems?

José's church brought a busload of junior and senior highers to hear a well-known Christian singer. As the kids emptied out of the bus, José looked around.

Some of the older girls and boys walked together. José watched them talking and laughing, looking sure of themselves. *I wish*— Unwilling to finish the thought, even to himself, José pushed it away.

José and his friend Ty followed Kevin, the youth leader, and his wife, Lyn, into the auditorium. Seats were filling up fast. Kevin turned and called out to the kids. "If we can't sit together, meet here at the end of the concert!"

Kevin was right. They had to split up. José and Ty found themselves down near the front, two rows away from the other kids. Listening to the excited talk all around him, José felt lonely again. *I bet if I had more friends, I'd always feel good inside.*

Soon the concert began. The music was great. Often the audience clapped along with the beat. Before long, José forgot about himself. After a number of songs, the singer started telling about how he'd come to know Jesus.

As he described his past sinful life, José felt uncomfortable. *Is there something wrong with me?* He wondered. *I don't have a very exciting testimony.*

"Accept Jesus, and all your problems will be over," the singer said.

Now José felt really confused. *I've already accepted Jesus, and I still have problems. Is there something I didn't do right?*

All around José, kids began standing up and going forward. One minute José wanted to join them; the next he felt as if his feet wouldn't move. *Should I go forward again?* he wondered. *Didn't I really accept Jesus?*

Instead of moving, José sat there. *I want to be a Christian, but I'm afraid to ask someone if I am. They'll think I'm dumb if I don't know.*

Finally José bowed his head. "Help me, Jesus," he prayed. "I really want to know where I'm at."

At the end of the concert, José stood up and slowly walked out. As he reached the outside door, he found his youth leader, Kevin. Hoping for a chance to talk but scared to try, José went over and waited beside him.

As kids poured out of the building, José stood there. At last he worked up the courage to begin. "Kevin—"

Just then, someone grabbed Kevin's arm and started talking. Then the crowd moved on, out toward the street.

When José climbed onto the bus, he followed Kevin and sat down next to him. On the ride back to church, José tried again. "Kevin, the singer said that if I became a Christian, all my problems would be over. But they aren't!"

"Are you confused?" Kevin asked. "I'm glad you spoke up. The singer didn't explain that very well. He should have said, 'If you accept Jesus, He'll be *with you* in your problems.' "

Whew! José felt as if the Empire State Building had fallen off his back.

"Have you found that's true since you asked Jesus to be your Savior?"

José thought about it for a moment and nodded. "Yeah, that's what it's been. But when the singer talked about how he was before he became a Christian, I thought—"

"That maybe you haven't been sinful enough?" As the bus passed under a streetlight, Kevin grinned. "I know. When I hear testimonies, I sometimes wonder that myself. But do you know something? You and I haven't gone through all the suffering that comes with the kind of sin he talked about. We don't have to have a colorful past life. It's exciting to be sheltered by God and become a Christian without that suffering."

"He explained it in a different way—the singer, I mean."

"Did you wonder if you needed to go forward again?" Kevin asked.

José nodded.

"Sometimes that happens. Different speakers use different ways of explaining how to receive salvation. But when Lyn and I prayed with you, you told Jesus you were sorry for your sins and asked forgiveness. You asked Him to be your Savior and Lord. That's what's important. When you did that, you became a Christian."

"But . . ." José hesitated. "Sometimes I'm not sure. Sometimes I don't *feel* like I'm a Christian."

"If you believed what you were saying when you prayed

that prayer, you *are* a Christian," Kevin answered. "You can't depend on your feelings. You have to go by what God promises."

Kevin dug in the big pockets of his jacket and pulled out a small Bible and flashlight. When he found the place he wanted, he turned the Bible toward José. "Read this."

Just then, someone spoke to Kevin and he turned away. José looked down and started reading. Suddenly the words were so real that they seemed written just for him: *"I write these things to you who believe in the name of the Son of God so that you may* know *that you have eternal life. . . ."* In Kevin's Bible the word *know* was underlined.

José took a deep breath, then let it out. All around him, the bus was noisy, but in José's spirit there was something steady and quiet. All the confusion he had felt fell away.

Snapping off the flashlight, José sat there, not wanting to talk with anyone. Silently he prayed. "I asked you, Jesus. I asked you to be my Savior and Lord. So you are! Thank you!"

In that moment José had a surprising new thought. *I'm going to have more and more friends. And someday maybe even a girlfriend. But that isn't what counts now.*

No one had ever told him, but José knew. *Jesus is the only one who can fill every empty space in my heart!*

TO **TALK** ABOUT

▸ Who is the only person who gives you the power to change your life? How is this possible?

▸ Has Jesus promised to take away all your problems? What has He promised instead?

- What does it mean to say, "Jesus will be with you in your problems"?

- **Remember Jesus and His big footprints? If you ask Him, He'll stay beside you every moment of the day or night.** In what ways would you like to have Jesus help you?

- **Jesus has already walked all the way to the cross for you.** Do you need to become a Christian? If so, you may want to pray something like this: "Jesus, I'm sorry for my sin. I believe you died on the cross for my sin, and I ask you to forgive me. I ask you to be my Savior and Lord. Thank you for my salvation!"

- Or do you need to know that because you've asked, you *have* received salvation? Why don't you read the verses from 1 John 5:1, 11–15 that José read on the bus? Ask Jesus to make himself real to you and thank him in faith.

To help you remember what Jesus has done for you and the choice you've made, write down your prayer in the empty space below or on the next page. Write the date and time and sign your name. Then, if you're reading this book by yourself, tell another Christian about the prayer you've prayed. It will seem more real to you.

This is what the Lord says.... "Fear not, for I have redeemed you; I have called you by name; you are mine. When you pass through the waters, I will be with you; and when you pass through the rivers, they will not sweep over you.... For I am the Lord your God, the Holy One of Israel, your Savior." Isaiah 43:1–3a

Thank you, Jesus, for your salvation for me. Thank you that I don't have to depend on my feelings. Give me the power to live by your promises.

Like a Porcupine

Danielle slammed the door of her locker. "What do you mean I'll get a bad grade?"

Jamie took a step backward. "Well, don't get mad at *me*. I'm just telling you what Mrs. Hernandez said. For each day your paper's late, it gets marked down."

"Aw, forget it!" answered Danielle. "I don't wanna hear about it."

"Hey, c'mon—"

"I said, forget it! You sound just like my mom."

Jamie tried again. "Hey, we're friends, remember? I was just trying to help. What's *really* bothering you?"

But Danielle was halfway down the hall. As she reached the outside door, she thought about the hurt look in Jamie's eyes.

Danielle turned and looked back. Jamie had started in the other direction. Instead of going after her, Danielle shrugged her shoulders and headed out the door.

Fifteen minutes later she dropped her books on the kitchen table. Mom was at the sink, peeling potatoes, and tried to give her a hug. But Danielle brushed Mom aside.

When Mom asked, "Did you have a nice day?" Danielle answered, "Fine, fine." As soon as she finished her cookies and milk, she headed upstairs to her room.

Half an hour later, Mom knocked on her door.

"Whadda you want?" Danielle answered.

"May I come in?" Mom asked through the door.

"Guess so," Danielle called back. "It's your house."

Slowly the door opened, and Mom came in. It was hard finding a place to sit down, but she managed. Picking up a pile of clothes, she cleared off a chair.

For a long moment, Mom was silent. Finally she asked, "How was your day?"

"Whadda you think?" Danielle answered from where she sprawled on the bed.

Mom tried again. "How do you feel about the way your day went?"

For Danielle it was like opening a faucet. All the awful things that had happened poured out. Starting from the moment she left home until she got back again, Danielle told everything that had gone wrong

Mom listened without speaking. Only once, when Danielle stopped, did she say, "I don't know what you mean. Will you explain again?"

At last Danielle finished by saying, "Even my best friend doesn't understand. Even Jamie—" Afraid the tears would come, Danielle broke off.

Mom's voice was gentle. "Danielle, how do you feel on the inside?"

"On the inside?"

"You told me all the awful things that happened to you today. But how do you *feel* about what happened?"

Danielle thought for a moment. "I feel mad," she said. "Stupid. Like I'm not worth anything. I'd like to hit back. Get even."

"You feel like a porcupine?" Mom asked.

Danielle almost smiled. She knew what Mom meant. Last summer they'd seen a porcupine cross a country road. Its quills stuck out in all directions. The end of those quills had barbs that would stay in whatever flesh they touched. Whoever was on the receiving end of a porcupine's quills felt pain.

"Like a porcupine." Danielle thought about it. For the first time she wondered, *Is it the stuff around me that's awful? Or the way I feel about everything?* Danielle still felt ready to throw quills at everyone.

"I'm glad you told me how you feel," Mom said. "You know, the feelings you have aren't right or wrong. It's what you do about your feelings that can be right or wrong. You make the choice about whether you're going to let your feelings control you."

Mom smiled. "Do you want to stay like a porcupine? Or do you want to learn to handle your feelings in a good way? Like right now. Why do you feel so grumpy?"

Danielle thought about it. Mom waited. Finally, Danielle spoke in a low voice. "I guess I woke up grumpy this morning. I was mad at you last night, and I felt the same way when I woke up."

"Can you tell me some of the things that made you angry?" asked Mom.

"Sure!" Danielle jumped at the chance. She sat up and faced Mom. "Sometimes you expect too much of me. Other times you treat me like a little kid."

As Danielle continued, Mom listened without speaking. Once she flinched, and a hurt look entered her eyes. In a moment it disappeared.

When at last Danielle finished, Mom said, "Tonight after supper, let's make a list. We'll decide what both of us think would be the right amount of work. You tell me what you feel you can handle, and we'll talk about it, okay?"

Mom paused. "Something else is happening. Things that never used to upset you bother you now. Sometimes you feel moody and grumpy, or really angry. Other times you're at the top of a mountain. Everything in the whole world seems wonderful."

Danielle thought about it. "I guess you're right."

"Your body is changing," Mom went on. "The way you think and feel about things is changing. Some of the things you used to like doing seem like kid stuff now. Do you know what I mean when I say that your emotions swing back and forth?"

Danielle nodded. "My moods go up and down."

"That's something that happens to both boys and girls your age. As a girl, you may notice the feeling more just before your period."

Danielle knew that was true. She felt relieved. "Do you have up-and-down days, too?"

"All of us do," Mom told her. "Sometimes we know what causes positive or negative feelings. A sunny day or bright colors make most of us feel better. And there are lots of reasons for feeling upset. Someone may say something that hurt you, or you're too tired, or—"

"Sometimes I don't know why I feel this way."

"Sometimes you *won't* know why," Mom answered. "That's okay. But grumpy moods are something all of us need to fight."

Just then Danielle remembered the hurt look in Jamie's eyes. *I wonder how she feels about the way I treated her.*

"Do you think you'd feel better about yourself if you learned some ways to handle your moods?" Mom asked. When Danielle didn't answer, Mom stood up. "Why don't you think about it for a while?"

As Mom headed for the door, Danielle wanted to reach out for a hug, the way she used to. Instead she said, "I didn't think you'd understand."

Mom came back. "I do, Danielle. I really do." Leaning down, Mom gave her a hug.

For a long time, Danielle lay on her bed thinking. The next day, when she saw Jamie again, Danielle was still thinking. But Jamie didn't look too happy to see her.

In that moment Danielle felt ashamed. *She's my friend. But she doesn't know how I'll treat her—if I'll be mean or nice.*

Seeing herself in that way didn't make Danielle feel good. *I guess I better do something about fighting my grumpy moods,* she thought. And she did.

TO **TALK** ABOUT

▸ What do you think Danielle did about the way she had treated Jamie?

▸ What does it mean to feel like a porcupine? To act like one? Explain.

▸ Why was it important for Danielle to talk about how she felt? Are feelings right or wrong? What *is* right or wrong?

▸ What if Danielle's mom had said, "You shouldn't feel that way?" What do you think Danielle would have done?

▸ When Danielle comes home from school in an angry mood, she can warn her family by saying, "I feel . . ." and finish the sentence with a feeling word like *mad, upset,* or *cranky*. Pretend you're Danielle. What would you say?

▸ What does it mean to say, "Grumpy moods are something we all have to fight"? Explain your ideas.

▸ In what ways can Danielle learn to handle her down moods? You can help her by finishing these sentences:
   If she's swamped with homework, she can say, "I feel . . ."
   If she's angry, she can say, "I feel . . ."
   If she's hurt, she can say, "I feel . . ."
   If she thinks kids are picking on her more than she can handle, she can say, "I feel . . ."

▸ To handle moods it also helps to do other things:
   If Danielle is cranky because she's tired, she can . . .
   If she wants to be alone for a while, she can . . .
   If she needs to forgive someone, she can . . .
   Instead of continuing to think about how bad she feels, Danielle can . . .
   If she needs exercise, she can . . .

▸ In what ways do *you* get rid of your grumpy moods?

▸ Sometimes people say, "Don't go out the door when you're angry." The Bible puts it this way: **"Do not let the sun go down while you are still angry, and do not give the devil a foothold."** Why is it a good idea to *not* go out the door when you're angry? To *not* let the sun go down without working things out? If you stay angry, how does that give the devil a foothold? Explain.

▸ Whenever you're hurt and upset, Jesus stands with His arms open to you. Is the way you think about yourself based on your feelings or on God's love? Why is it important to know the difference?

▸ **Remember Jesus and His big footprints? If you ask Him, He will walk right alongside of you. Ask Him to give you all the power of His Holy Spirit to help you handle your moods. Then work with Him by doing your part.**

"In your anger do not sin": Do not let the sun go down while you are still angry, and do not give the devil a foothold.
Ephesians 4:26–27

Jesus, you know my body is changing. Often I have up-and-down moods. Help me handle my moods in a strong way. I want to be a fun person to be around.

Monty's Question

As Monty entered the Christian school he attended, he remembered the news he'd seen that morning. The TV broadcast talked about a well-known athlete who had died of AIDS.

Monty felt uneasy. All this talk about AIDS, and he didn't quite understand it. *Will I get AIDS, too?* he wondered. He didn't like that idea one bit.

On his way down a long hall, Monty tried to push his worried thoughts aside. But his question returned in health class.

Sometimes Mr. Robinson's topics embarrassed Monty. Often he wanted to disappear through the floor. But today his teacher started out by saying, "I want to talk with you about AIDS."

Around Monty the kids stopped wiggling. The room grew quiet.

"AIDS stands for Acquired Immune Deficiency Syndrome. Those are big words. Can someone tell me what your *immune system* is?"

When Mr. Robinson called on him, Monty felt glad they had studied that. "It's what keeps me well," he said. "It's like having soldiers fight against the germs that try to make me sick."

"Good!" said the teacher. "Now, let's say you were exposed to a cold. If your immune system worked well, what would happen?"

"I probably wouldn't get the cold," answered Monty.

"But what if your system didn't work?"

"I'd get sick."

Mr. Robinson nodded. "A person with AIDS has a virus that attacks the immune system, so it doesn't work well. That person easily gets a cold or flu or anything else. And usually that person gets more ill, even with something like a cold, than someone who doesn't have AIDS."

Mr. Robinson looked around the room. "Can someone tell me what happens to people who have AIDS?"

Several kids answered at once. "They die."

"We all die sometime," Mr. Robinson answered. "But people with AIDS die sooner. Sometimes people carry the HIV virus that causes AIDS for many years before realizing they have it. They're called carriers and can infect other people, even though they don't know they're sick.

"Once someone gets the virus, there's no way to get rid of it. Often people with AIDS die from illnesses they get because their immune system doesn't work in a normal way."

Inside Monty the scary feeling was back. *Will I get AIDS?* he asked himself again.

Mr. Robinson went on. "There's no one who wants AIDS. So we need to know how people get it."

"Only gays get AIDS," blurted out a boy in the back of the room.

"Gays?" asked another boy.

"He's talking about people who have a homosexual relationship," Mr. Robinson. "If you wonder about that, why don't you ask one of your parents or another grown-up you trust? They'll help you with any questions you have.

"It's true that many homosexuals do get AIDS," Mr. Robinson went on. "But the general population has also been affected."

Monty leaned forward to listen. This was exactly what he wanted to know.

"Some people have become sick with AIDS because of a blood transfusion. In this country our medical people work hard to give us a clean blood supply. But it's still a concern for all of us."

Mr. Robinson started listing the causes of AIDS on the board. "Newborn babies may have AIDS because their mothers were infected. The babies are innocent victims, and it's really hard to see their suffering. But as you grow older, you need to know there are ways you can avoid getting AIDS."

Mr. Robinson added to the list. "Some people get infected by sharing a dirty needle with someone who shoots drugs. If you don't use drugs, you don't have to worry about getting AIDS that way.

"You can't get AIDS by touching or being around someone who has the virus, but you can get it through sexual contact. We've already learned about sexual intercourse. It belongs in the relationship between a husband and wife. The Bible tells us that God doesn't want you to have sexual intercourse unless you're married. If you do get married, He wants you to be faithful to your husband or wife.

"If you and the person you love wait with sexual intercourse until marriage, you offer each other a special gift. You have lived the way God wants you to live. But you're also less likely to be carriers of disease."

Mr. Robinson looked around the room. "Sometimes people think they can get by with stretching the rules. They think, 'Only once won't hurt.' But it's possible to get AIDS by having sex only once with an infected person.

"One of the most important things you can do is to live your Christian beliefs. When others tempt you to have sexual intercourse, say no. When someone says, 'Everybody's doing it!' say 'I'm *not* doing it!' You'll be living the way God wants you to live. You'll also be less likely to get AIDS."

Again Mr. Robinson looked around the room. "Any questions?"

For a long moment Monty waited. *How would I feel if I got AIDS?* he wondered. He imagined how awful it would be to think, *I'm gonna get worse and worse until I die.*

Monty was afraid to ask, but the idea of being that sick bothered him. Finally he raised his hand. "How should we act toward people who have AIDS?"

"That's an important question," answered Mr. Robinson. "It shows you're doing some good thinking. We need to pray for people with AIDS. We need to be kind to them, the way we are to anyone who is sick and hurting. They need care and love like everyone else.

"But at the same time, we shouldn't say that a sexual lifestyle that spreads AIDS and other diseases is okay. It's not. In the Bible God gives us clear guidelines for how He wants us to act. He tells us to be a holy people.

"Any more questions?" For a moment Mr. Robinson waited. When no one spoke up, he erased the list on the board and said, "I have a quiz for you. I want to be sure all of you understand what I've told you."

As Monty picked up his pencil, he realized that the scared feeling in his stomach was gone. *I'm glad I have some choices,* he thought. *I'm glad I can choose how I want to live.*

TO **TALK** ABOUT

▸ What started Monty thinking about AIDS?

▸ In what ways do people get the virus that causes AIDS? Can you get AIDS just by being around someone who has it?

▸ What happens to people with the AIDS virus? What happens to their immune system?

▸ How should we treat people who have AIDS?

▸ As you get older, you'll need to make a choice. How can saying no to sex outside of marriage lessen your risk of getting AIDS? Explain.

▸ When kids want someone to do something wrong, they often say, "Everybody's doing it." Think of a way in which you are tempted. Is it really true that everybody is doing it? How do you know?

▸ Even if a lot of kids *are* doing something wrong, does that mean *you* should do it? Give reasons for your answer.

▸ How can you help other kids be strong?

▸ Jesus wants all of us to walk in His footsteps and be pure. Talk with your mom or dad about what it means to be pure.

▸ **If you want to be like Jesus, ask Him to help you grow up strong in Him. Ask Him to give you** *all* **the power of His Holy Spirit to help you make choices that please Him. Then understand that even though you ask for the Holy Spirit's help, you yourself still have to make the right choices.** One of them will be to say "No!" if someone you especially like tempts you to spend time in a place where the two of you are alone. Instead, choose to have fun with groups of Christian kids that help you stay true to how Jesus wants you to live.

May the God who gives us peace make you holy in every way and keep your whole being—spirit, soul, and body—free from every fault at the coming of our Lord Jesus Christ. He who calls you will do it, because he is faithful. 1 Thessalonians 5:23-24 (TEV)

Lord Jesus, I want to live the way you did when you were here on earth. I want to be clean and pure and holy in everything I do and think. In your name I ask for all the power of your Holy Spirit to be wise and make the right choices. Thank you!

Country Cousin

That morning Jenny had come into the city on the train. Jenny lived on a farm and hadn't seen her cousin Erica for over two years. Now they would have a whole week of fun together.

The first thing Jenny noticed was how much Erica had changed since the last time they were together. *Wow!* Jenny thought. *Does she ever look cute!* Jenny especially liked Erica's jeans.

That afternoon they were off to a good start. Some boys dropped over to see Erica. Jenny especially liked Ross. As he left he told her, "See you tonight, Jenny!"

Erica's friends from school had planned a party for that evening. Jenny could hardly wait. As soon as the boys left, she followed her cousin upstairs to figure out what to wear.

Jenny's half-open suitcase lay on the floor of Erica's bedroom. As Jenny started taking out her clothes, Erica stopped her. "Wait a minute," she said.

Erica pulled open a door. Jenny had never seen such a full closet. Jeans, tops, and dresses were packed in as tight as they could go. On the floor beneath the clothes lay a jumble of shoes.

"We're almost the same size," Erica said. "Maybe I've got something you can wear."

Great! Jenny hardly dared hope. *If I dress like Erica, maybe Ross will really like me.*

Erica started at one end of the closet, pulling out tops and then jeans. One by one Jenny tried them on. She liked one pair of jeans especially.

Erica walked around her. "Nope," she said. "They're too high on your hips."

"That's how I always wear 'em," answered Jenny.

But Erica kept looking. Soon she came up with another pair. "Try these. They'll fit better."

Jenny pulled them on. The waist had a lower cut than what she usually wore.

Erica inspected her again. "They're perfect. That's how they're supposed to fit. And wear this top—it'll go great with those jeans."

Jenny pulled on the top she knew would be too small. *It doesn't even reach the waist of these jeans!* Yet she didn't dare tell Erica how uncomfortable she felt. More than anything, she wanted to look as grown-up as Erica did.

"Yup!" Erica walked around Jenny once more. "Now you look like one of us."

Well, then it's worth it, Jenny told herself. *That's what I want—to look like a city girl.*

But when Jenny saw herself in the mirror, she felt uneasy. *I'm glad Mom and Dad won't see me. They'd be upset.* Aloud she asked, "You're sure these clothes aren't too small?"

Erica laughed as though that was the funniest thing she'd ever heard.

Again Jenny pushed her uneasiness aside. *It'll be fun looking as cute as Erica.*

Soon it was time to leave, and the two girls set off down the street. The party was only two blocks away at Carmen's house.

As Jenny and Erica waited to cross the street, a car wheeled around the corner. The driver honked and waved. Jenny waved back.

Brakes squealed, and the driver backed up the car. Three boys leaned out of the windows to talk. They looked at least five years older then Jenny and Erica.

Jenny hung back, letting Erica do all the talking. At first Jenny felt shy, then uncomfortable, then almost scared. There was something about these boys she didn't like.

Finally one of them asked, "Wanna go for a ride?"

Erica shook her head. "Nah, but thanks. We're headed for a party down the street."

As the boys pulled away, they asked Erica's name, and she gave it to them. Revving up the engine, the driver called out, "Well, see ya around!"

"You mean you didn't know them?" asked Jenny as the car pulled away from the curb.

"Of course not! Never saw them before in my life!"

"Then why did you talk to them?"

Erica looked at Jenny as though she'd asked the most stupid question in the world. "Hey, you're the one who waved."

"At home we wave at everyone," Jenny answered. "When

they honked, I thought you knew them. How come they stopped?"

Erica smirked. "They just liked the way we looked."

Jenny's heart thudded down to her toes. *So that's it! That's why she didn't want me wearing my own jeans.*

Suddenly all the beautiful clothes in Erica's closet didn't mean very much. To Jenny they seemed like a bunch of junk—junk that made her cousin look the wrong way.

Sure, I want to look nice, Jenny thought. *I want to look like the other kids. But . . .*

Jenny looked down at her outfit and didn't like herself very much. In fact, she felt ashamed. She didn't like what she was saying through the clothes she wore.

She thought about Ross and wanting to dress so he'd like her. But then Jenny knew. *I'm dressing to get attention by the way I look instead of by being the person I am.*

When Jenny breathed deep, the button at her waist popped off. "Oh, wow! I can't go to the party this way."

"Aw, c'mon," Erica said. "No one will notice. We'll find a pin when we get there."

In that split second, Jenny knew it wouldn't work to explain to her cousin. "Why don't you go to the party? I'll run back and take care of it."

"Well . . ."

"I know where Carmen's house is," Jenny said quickly. "I was there last time I visited you. Go on! I'll catch up."

Before Erica could say another word, Jenny hurried off. As soon as she reached her cousin's bedroom, she pulled her best jeans and favorite top from the suitcase and changed into them.

It's not whether I live in the country or the city, Jenny decided. *It's the kind of person I want to be.*

For a moment she stood in front of the full-length mirror. *I look nice,* she thought, feeling surprised.

When Jenny reached the party, Ross had been looking for her. Something in his grin gave him away.

He likes me the way I am. Jenny smiled. *And I like myself, too!*

TO **TALK** ABOUT

▸ What did Jenny mean when she decided, "It's not whether I live in the country or the city. It's the kind of person I want to be"?

▸ Whether you're a boy or a girl, what do clothes tell other people about the kind of person you are?

▸ What did Erica want to say through the way she dressed? What did Jenny want to say?

▸ Why do kids want to wear clothes that are the same as what other kids wear? What's the difference between wearing clothes that are popular and clothes that give the wrong impression?

▸ If you make a choice like Jenny's or Erica's, what difference will it make in your life? How will your choices affect the kind of friends you make?

▸ A certain type of clothing might be worn by gang members or reflect someone's negative thoughts or beliefs. Why is it important to avoid those kinds of clothes?

‣ Is it necessary to wear trendy clothes in order to look nice? Why or why not?

‣ Sometimes it's hard to know if a person is a boy or a girl. Why is it important for girls to look like girls and boys to look like boys? What does the way you look tell others about how you feel about yourself?

‣ If you're a girl, how can warm, attractive colors and feminine clothing show that you enjoy being a girl? Give reasons for what you think.

‣ Whether you're a boy or a girl, think about the clothes you choose. What do they say about you? Explain.

‣ **When Jesus walked on earth, He made clear footprints. We know what He believed and how He wanted to live.** Are there ways in which you need to make clear footprints? Ways in which you need to show others what you believe? What are they?

Your beauty should consist of your true inner self, the greatless beauty of a gentle and quiet spirit, which is of the greatest value in God's sight. 1 Peter 3:4 (TEV)

Jesus, I don't want to feel out of it with kids because of the way I dress. But I don't want to be an embarrassment to you, either. Help me to dress in a way that honors you.

Lauren Waits

On that Friday morning in July, Lauren sat in the kitchen, putting on nail polish. When the phone rang, she thought, *It won't be for me,* and kept on with her nails.

But the phone kept ringing, and her older sister, Sabrina, called out, "Will you get it, Lauren? I'm in the tub."

Lauren sighed and took her time about getting to the phone. "Hello?" she said. She was right, of course. It was for Sabrina.

The minute Sabrina knew it was Kirk, she was out of the tub, into a bathrobe, and at the phone. "Tonight? Right. That'll be fun. See you at six-thirty."

As she hung up, Sabrina glowed. "Do you know what? Do you know who that was?"

"Yup, I know," answered Lauren, not feeling very excited. As far as she was concerned, it was just one more boy on Sabrina's list.

"Kirk is the greatest guy in the whole school! And he asked me out!"

Lauren tried to pretend that she cared, but her smile felt

stiff. She was glad when her sister left to get dressed. *Always Sabrina,* she thought. *Always, always, always. Sure, Mom says I'm too young to go out with boys. But even when I'm older, who will ask me? What if I never get any dates?*

Just thinking about the way Sabrina looked, Lauren sighed again. On a shelf above the sink were two pictures: Sabrina—slender and lovely, long dark hair blowing in the wind. *Then there's me,* Lauren thought. *Skinny legs. Mousy hair. Chest like a boy.* As she bent her head to finish her nails, Lauren blinked away tears.

In that instant she remembered the slumber party that night. *Well, at least I can go to Rachel's. She's still my best friend.*

Just then the phone rang, and Lauren picked it up again.

"Hi there!" said a warm voice on the other end of the line.

"Hey, Aunt Mickey!" Something in Lauren jumped, just hearing the voice of her favorite aunt. Mickey was Mom's youngest sister. She had never married and was a social worker who lived almost 200 miles away.

"Just found out I need to come your way tonight to pick up a runaway girl," Mickey told her. "How about if I stay overnight? Then we can talk before I have to leave in the morning. How does that sound?"

"Sabrina has a date," Lauren answered. "Mom isn't here, but I'm sure it'll be okay with her."

The moment the words were out, Lauren felt uneasy. *Will it* really *be okay with Mom?* she wondered. After Dad had left them, Mom started dating. Often she had even more dates than Sabrina.

But Lauren pushed her uneasiness aside. "It'll be great to have you come!" she said to Mickey. "We haven't seen you for a long time."

"I know. I'm lonesome for you, too. I'm not sure exactly when I'll be there, but probably around seven, okay?"

"Terrific!"

As Lauren got off the phone, she felt good just thinking about Mickey. Her aunt's name was really Michelle, but when she was little, Lauren started calling her Mickey. The name had stuck, just like the special relationship between them.

Lauren's sister wasn't happy to hear about Mickey coming. "I have a date, you know."

"I know. I told her. You don't have to be here." Then Lauren remembered. "Oh wow! I have a slumber party at Rachel's tonight. Mom will have to take care of Mickey."

But when Mom got home from work, she said, "I can't be here. I've got a dinner date."

"Aw, Mom!" Lauren told her. "You're always going out. Can't you change it to another night?"

Mom shook her head. "Nope. You told my sis she could come. You take care of her. I've got only an hour to get ready."

"But I'm supposed to go to Rachel's!" Lauren wailed. "Can't Mickey go out to eat with you?"

Lauren wasn't surprised that Mom didn't like that idea. "Let's just leave a key for her," Mom said. "Mickey can come in and go to bed early. She won't mind."

Soon Sabrina and Mom left, and Lauren got ready for Rachel's. She had everything in her knapsack when she wondered how Aunt Mickey would feel coming into an empty house. *It'll be worse than when I'm all alone. Mickey doesn't know anyone around here.*

Since Dad left, Lauren had been alone a lot. She thought about it. *Even though I'd rather be at Rachel's, it's not fair. Mickey's nice.*

Inside, Lauren felt torn, wanting to treat her aunt the way Mickey always treated her. Yet, even more, Lauren wanted to be at the slumber party. *Here I am, home alone again. Everyone but me having a date.*

Then Lauren remembered how Aunt Mickey always managed to laugh about something. Now Lauren tried to laugh, but it didn't work. Taking her knapsack up to her room, she dropped it in a corner with her sleeping bag. Then she called Rachel and said she wasn't coming.

After an hour of waiting, Lauren wondered if it was worth it. *Maybe Mickey won't show up.* Just thinking about that possibility, Lauren felt disappointed. At the same time, she wanted to go to the party.

Finally Lauren went back to her room and picked up her knapsack and sleeping bag. The next moment she dropped them again. *Mickey's never broken a promise.* That was one of the things Lauren liked about her.

Just then a car door slammed. Lauren hurried to a front window. Sure enough, it was Mickey!

Lauren ran down the stairs and out the door. She threw herself into Mickey's arms.

"Hey, there! Good to see you!" Mickey held Lauren out for a long look. "Wow! What a lovely grown-up person you've become!"

"I'm grown-up?" Lauren felt afraid to hope. She didn't

dare believe the rest of it. "And lovely besides?"

A smile spread across Mickey's face. "You sure are! I like your hair that way. And you still give a wonderful hug!"

"Thanks," Lauren said gratefully. Mickey hadn't changed. She had the same dark hair Mom used to have. And Mickey's eyes were warm and caring. Lauren knew that Mickey was a Christian and wondered if that's why she was so nice.

Lauren helped Mickey bring her bag into the house. As she looked around, Mickey asked, "Your mom and Sabrina are gone? They both have dates?"

"Yeah," Lauren answered. "Sorry about that." She felt embarrassed that neither of them had tried to change their plans, since Mickey came so seldom.

"Well, then, let's celebrate that you and I are together," Mickey said. "Let's go out to eat somewhere. Somewhere really nice, okay?"

In a few minutes they were off. For the first time since she'd seen Mickey a year ago, Lauren talked without stopping. There was something about her aunt that made Lauren feel she could tell her anything.

They went to a country inn, and it was fun to be in such a nice place. It was even more fun to talk, just the two of them. But when they were having dessert, Mickey asked, "Lauren, how are you *really* doing?"

Lauren blinked with surprise and tried to hold back the tears. When they came anyway, Mickey waited until Lauren could speak. It took three tries before she said, "Mickey, do you ever feel like a zero?"

Mickey laughed, and Lauren felt sorry she'd asked. But

when Mickey answered, her voice was soft. "Lots of times. Lots and lots of times. You see, I have a good-looking older sister, too."

In spite of herself, Lauren smiled through her tears.

"And lots of times I thought I'd *never* be asked out."

"You really thought that?"

"I really thought that."

"But you were . . . I mean, you *have* been—" Lauren broke off, not wanting to hurt her aunt.

"Not much in high school," Mickey said. "Boys always asked your mom. But later on, yes, when they started looking for a wife."

She winked. "They think I'm good wife material."

"But you haven't gotten married."

"And I'm not sorry. Some people feel sorry for me, I'm sure, but that's their problem. It's not mine."

"How come? I mean, why haven't you gotten married?"

"So far I haven't felt that God put me together with the right man," Mickey said. "It's much better *not* to marry than to marry the wrong person."

"But do you ever feel like you're—" Again Lauren stopped.

"Like I'm not worth anything? Like I'm not cute or worth being with?" Mickey grinned, but her eyes were serious. "You know, Lauren, it can be really fun to find the right person at the right time. But it isn't *all* there is to life. Sometimes girls do wrong things because they think it's a way to get dates. It never works—not in the long run."

Mickey set down her iced tea. "I don't want to spend my life looking under every bush or around every corner for a man. If God wants me to marry, He'll show me who the person should be. But if He *doesn't* want me to marry, that's okay. It's okay to *not* get married.

"I have a full life," Mickey went on. "And I'm doing new, fun things all the time. Because I don't have a family, there are ways in which I'm free to help other people. But you see, if I'm married or not married, I'm still a whole person—a person valued by God."

"Do you ever get lonely?" Lauren asked.

"Sure," Mickey told her. "Times like that I try to reach out to others—to see if there's a way I can help them. Times like that I come and see you."

Lauren grinned. "And take me out for supper."

"I'm taking you? Oops!" Mickey laughed. "Better see if I have enough money."

In that moment Lauren felt glad she'd skipped the slumber party. But it wasn't until they returned home that Mickey discovered what had happened. When she went into Lauren's bedroom, she saw the stuffed knapsack and sleeping bag and asked, "Were you going somewhere?"

Lauren had never lied to Mickey, and she didn't want to start. But when she answered Mickey's question, she wasn't prepared for the tears that came to her aunt's eyes.

"Lauren, I'm glad that you were here when I came."

"Me too," Lauren said.

"I'm glad to know you're still the kind of person you are," Mickey went on. "Keep on being that way, okay?"

Lauren nodded. "I'll try."

"But it's getting late, and I have a long drive tomorrow. I really need a good night's sleep. Couldn't you still go to the slumber party? You'll stay up all night talking, won't you?"

Again Lauren nodded, her thoughts already jumping ahead to the fun she could have.

"I'll drive you there, okay?" Mickey asked.

This time it was Lauren's turn to feel tears in her eyes. *Wow! I get to do* both *things!* She hugged her aunt so tight that Mickey squealed.

TO **TALK** ABOUT

▶ What were some of the things that bothered Lauren about her sister, Sabrina? In what ways was Sabrina acting like her mother?

▶ What kind of person do you think Mickey was? How can you tell from the story?

▶ So far, Mickey had chosen not to marry. She said, "I'm a whole person." What does it mean to be a whole person? How did Mickey feel about her life?

▶ **Every one of us needs to know it's okay to be what we are.** In what ways did Mickey give Lauren that message?

▶ What did you like about the relationship between Lauren and Mickey? How did they help each other? What miracle do you think Lauren experienced in the way she felt about herself?

▶ Lauren wanted to go to the slumber party, yet she also wanted to be at home when Mickey arrived. Have you ever been torn between feeling you should do something and wanting to do something else? What happened?

▸ Lauren saw her mother and sister dating and thought it would be fun. Instead, Lauren learned a secret of the heart. What was that secret?

▸ What are some good things about being single? Have you thought about the fact that both Jesus and the apostle Paul were single? Does being single mean you have to be lonely? Why or why not? Do you think some married people are lonely?

▸ Mickey had accepted the way she was. She helped Lauren accept the way Lauren was. Whether you're a boy or a girl, is there some way you need to say, "It's okay to be what I am"? Explain what you mean.

▸ When we feel happy with who we are and the way God created us, we also feel free to grow in ways that would help us. Think of a way you have grown in your ability to do something. What is it? How can you give that ability to Jesus?

"The King [Jesus] will reply, 'I tell you the truth, whatever you did for one of the least of these brothers of mine, you did for me.' " Matthew 25:40

You know what, God? When I compare myself with some-one else, I feel sorry for ME. In the name of your Son, Jesus, I choose to accept and be glad for the way you made me. Help me think about the feelings of others.

Travis
Thinks Ahead

As Travis looked down from the stands, his older brother ran onto the field. Just watching him, Travis felt proud. *It's not every kid who has a football hero for a brother.*

A junior in high school, Riley was already over six feet tall. With surprisingly broad shoulders for his age, he was the best tight end Central had ever had.

When the team lined up, Travis and his friend Mark clapped and yelled with the crowd.

"Bet Riley will score big again," Mark said.

The whistle blew, and the ball snapped into play. Time after time, Riley was at exactly the right place at the right moment. As he caught the ball and completed a thirty-six-yard run, the crowd went wild.

Mark pounded Travis on the back. "Wow! Look at Riley! He's such a great player now. I wonder what he'll be like as a senior."

Around Travis, people leaned forward or turned to talk with him. Everyone said the same thing. "What an awesome brother you have!"

A wide grin on his face, Travis called back, "I know it!" But after a while, something inside Travis started to hurt.

During a lull, he looked around until he saw Mom and Dad in the stands. Dad's face was alive with excitement. Mom had a worry line between her eyebrows. Travis knew what she was thinking. Before every game she'd say, "I hope Riley doesn't get hurt!"

Dad also hoped Riley would be okay, but he loved football. For as long as Travis could remember, he and Dad and Riley had played in the backyard. *But Riley always catches the ball, and I always fumble,* Travis told himself. He'd been thinking about that a lot.

As the whistle blew, Travis turned back to the game. His thoughts kept pace with the players on the field. Dad wanted him in sports. Travis knew that soon Dad would talk about it again.

"You guys need exercise," he often said. Taking Dad at his word, Riley had gone out for football because that was the sport he liked best. But Travis wasn't sure what to do.

Riley's way out ahead of everyone, Travis thought. *I'm just not built the same way.*

As the second half started, Travis leaned forward. Elbows on his knees, he rested his chin on his hands and rubbed his cheeks. *Wonder when I'll start getting fuzz on my chin like Riley,* he thought.

Then Travis felt his forehead. *More zits! Every time I turn around, there's a gob of 'em!*

Just then Riley made a touchdown. Travis jumped up to clap and cheer with the rest. But his hurt was growing. *To everyone else Riley is the big hero. What's the use of try-ing to keep up?*

When the game finished, 24 to 14, Central had won, but Travis felt grumpy. Climbing down from the stands, he started off to meet Mom and Dad for the ride home. When he found them, they headed toward the car. But every few steps someone stopped them.

"Great son you have there!" one man called out. But Travis knew he meant Riley.

Dad waved and said thanks and kept walking. Soon another man stopped him. "He'll make big time in football, don't you think?"

Travis walked on ahead. It was always the same. *Riley this, Riley that. Riley, Riley, Riley.* The hurt inside Travis changed to an ache.

By the time he reached the car, he was quiet, but angry. When Dad said, "Let's go for pizza," Travis answered, "Let's not and say we did."

When Mom asked, "What's wrong, Travis?" he shrugged and didn't answer. For the next two days, Travis sulked around the house.

One minute he wanted to act better. The next minute he didn't. Then he felt mad at himself. Finally he wheeled his bike out of the garage and took off on a long ride.

The wind felt good on his face. It wasn't long before Travis felt better. It was as though he could think again.

I'll never be as good a football player as Riley. I don't have the same build. I'm not as strong. So why do I tell myself I have to play football?

Soon Travis went a step further in his thinking. *I can*

have fun playing football with just the guys. But I don't have to compete with Riley. What can I do instead?

By the time Travis biked six blocks, he had thought of several things. *Play golf? Too much money, unless I caddy. Jog? Go out for track? Well, maybe. Cross-country ski?*

Then it hit him. He really liked batting a tennis ball around a court and playing with anyone he could find. Before now, it never seemed important. In this moment it seemed earthshaking.

I can play tennis!

Slamming on his brakes, Travis spun his bike around. For the first time all week he felt excited.

The minute Dad got home from work, Travis pounced on him. "Can I buy a good tennis racket? And maybe take lessons?"

"Hmm." Dad looked surprised. Then he thought about it. "You know, that might be a really great choice. And there's a good court right near our house."

"I could join the tennis club at school," Travis said.

"And if you stay healthy, you can play tennis the rest of your life."

Soon Travis started playing every day. At first his friend Mark usually beat him. Then Travis started winning more and more games. But soon he decided it would be fun to compete with himself. He began setting goals in what he could learn.

As he looked in the mirror one day, Travis grinned at himself. His body was changing. His arms and shoulders were getting stronger. And he had fewer zits. *Maybe all the exercise helps!*

One day his brother, Riley, came to watch Travis play. "Way to go!" Riley called out. "Lookin' good!"

Travis felt warmed by Riley's praise. Most of all, Travis felt good about himself.

to **TALK** about

▸ **Many of us compare our weaknesses with some-one else's strengths.** How did Travis feel about his own body whenever he thought of Riley?

▸ In what way did Travis think ahead? Why was his choice an especially good one for him? If there wasn't a way to play tennis, what other sports could Travis choose?

▸ What are some team sports in which kids in your area take part? What are some good reasons for taking part in team sports?

▸ Individual sports are ones in which a person can be active without depending on a group. If people are healthy, they are able to take part in such sports for most of their lives. Name some of these sports.

▸ If you're active in team sports, why can it be good to also enjoy a sport that doesn't depend on a team?

▸ With many sports it's necessary to compete with other kids. How can that be helpful? How can that be hurtful? **If you're involved in a competitive sport, how can you compete with yourself instead of competing**

----

with other kids? Explain. How can improving in a sport be a reward in itself?

▸ How can taking care of your body through eating well and regular exercise be a way to honor God?

[God said,] "So do not fear, for I am with you; do not be dismayed, for I am your God. I will strengthen you and help you, I will uphold you with my righteous right hand." Isaiah 41:10

Help me, Lord, to honor you by taking good care of my body. Help me to take part in sports that give me the fun and exercise I need.

Through the Wall

After school Mindy went over to Erin's house. The day before, Erin's mother had brought a new baby home from the hospital.

First Erin held her little sister. Then her mom, Mrs. O'Neill, asked Mindy, "Do you want to hold the baby?"

Mindy felt scared. "What if I do something wrong?"

"I'll help you," she answered. "If you sit down in this big chair, I'll put her on your lap."

As Mindy held the baby, she forgot about being scared. "Look at all her red hair! And her cute little face!"

The baby's eyes were closed, and she slept peacefully. Mindy's arms tightened around her. It was the way she used to feel holding her favorite doll. Only this one breathed and was real.

"Ever since Erin was born, we've wanted another child," Mrs. O'Neill told Mindy. "We waited a long time."

After a few minutes the baby yawned, opened her eyes, and stretched her legs. Mrs. O'Neill pulled back the blanket so Mindy could see the baby's little feet.

Then she helped Mindy uncurl the baby's fist. "Look at her fingernails!" Mindy exclaimed. "They're just like mine, but so tiny!"

To Mindy the baby was a miracle. She loved Erin's sister. "Can I come back and see her tomorrow?" Mindy asked when she needed to leave.

When she reached home, it was time for supper. Her mom set the serving dishes on the table, and everyone sat down.

Dad asked the blessing, but then silence hung heavy over the table. As she ate, Mindy watched Dad, then Mom, then her sixteen-year-old sister. Twila was pushing green beans around her plate. Mom wasn't eating much, either. But Dad was eating twice as much as usual.

"What's wrong?" Mindy wanted to ask. She couldn't remember another meal when no one talked.

Mindy felt uncomfortable. *Are Mom and Dad mad?* she wondered. *Or do they feel bad about something?* Mindy wasn't sure.

Whatever it was, it was awful. And it had something to do with her sister. Twila sat there, just staring at her plate. Mom and Dad didn't even tell her to eat.

Finally Mindy could stand the silence no longer. "What's going on?" she asked. "What's the matter?"

"Mind your own business," Twila answered quickly.

Mom was silent, but her eyes pleaded, "Don't ask."

"We don't want to talk about it right now," Dad said. Mindy knew he wouldn't say more.

The minute supper was over, Twila went to her room. Things didn't get any better when she left. Mindy felt uneasy just being with Mom and Dad. Deep in their eyes, they looked hurt and sad and angry all at once. When Mindy went to bed, she still didn't know what was wrong.

She had been sleeping for a while when a sound woke her. For a moment Mindy lay still, trying to figure out what it was.

When the sound came again, Mindy realized it was voices coming through the heat vent in the wall between her bedroom and Mom and Dad's. As Mindy listened, the words blurred together. Dad's voice sounded sharp and angry.

What's going on? Mindy wondered for the hundredth time. Climbing out of bed, she huddled close to the wall. *Dad hardly ever gets mad.*

Twila's voice was louder now. "Don't yell at me! I said I'm sorry!"

Her voice softened, but the words came clear. "I'm sorry I got myself into this. I'm sorry I'm pregnant."

Mindy's heart raced. *My sister is going to have a baby? How can she have a baby when she isn't married?* Suddenly Mindy felt scared.

Twila's voice dropped low, sounding ashamed, but Mindy could still hear. "I'm sorry for what I did," Twila said. "I thought it would be fun, but it wasn't."

Mom's voice was low now, too, and Mindy couldn't pick out what she said. Then Twila spoke again.

"You were right, Mom, when you said it's important to wait to be married. I thought you were old-fashioned—that you didn't know what you were talking about—"

Twila's voice broke off. Even through the wall, Mindy heard her sobs.

"I'm sorry I hurt you, Mom. I'm sorry, Dad." For a long moment there was silence, broken only by weeping. Then Twila spoke again.

"I'll get an *abortion* so people don't find out."

"NO!" Dad exclaimed. The word exploded. "You will *not* get an abortion!"

An abortion? Mindy almost said the word aloud. She'd heard about abortions on TV, but her sister getting one?

Twila's voice had changed. "If I get an abortion, I won't have to have the baby. You won't have to be embarrassed. I know where I can go. I would have gone already if Mom hadn't caught on that I'm pregnant."

"You planned an *abortion*?" Mom's voice sounded sad and angry at the same time.

"Sure, Mom. It just takes a few minutes, and everything is all taken care of."

Just then Mindy remembered Erin's baby sister. The soft skin and red hair. The helpless little body. The tiny fingernails. The perfect toes.

Twila would kill a baby like that?

Deep inside Mindy the tears started. She tried to push them away, but they kept coming. As she knelt on the floor next to the wall, Mindy began to shake. Tears spilled over and ran down her cheeks.

Unable to listen anymore, Mindy grabbed her blanket and pulled it over her head. *A little baby like Erin's sister? Twila would kill a baby like that?*

When Mindy's sobs quieted, Twila was speaking again. "But if I have the baby, won't you be embarrassed?"

"That's not what's important," Mom said. "What you did

is wrong, and you'll have to live with the consequences. But we'll stick by you because we love you. We don't want you to make things even worse with an abortion."

"But girls say—"

"Twila—" Dad's voice was gentle now. "Other girls are going to tell you all kinds of things. When you stop a beating heart, you're destroying a life that God created. Do you really want to do that?"

"But what do I do with the baby?" Twila wailed.

"We'll keep talking about what you want to do," Mom said quietly. "There are special places where you can go—Christian homes where girls live while waiting for the birth of their baby. The people there will help you decide whether you want to keep your baby or place it for adoption."

"I'm scared, Mom. I don't know what to do." Twila sounded confused now. "I don't feel grown-up enough for all this."

"Right now you don't have to decide between keeping the baby and adoption," Mom told her. "But you *do* need to make the most important choice of all—to remember that your baby is a human life."

"And there's something else." Dad stopped, and it was Mom who explained.

"You also need to see a doctor and make sure the baby is okay and you're okay."

"Well, why wouldn't I be?" Twila sounded resentful again.

"If you have sex with someone who's had sex with some-one else, you can be exposed to a sexually transmitted disease."

Twila's wail came loud and clear through the wall. "I never believed all the awful things that could happen to me!"

When Twila started weeping again, it sounded like the whimpering of a young child. As Mindy listened, she wondered if Twila would ever be happy again.

Mindy crawled back into bed. For a long time, she lay awake thinking about Erin's baby sister.

TO **TALK** ABOUT

▸ When Erin's mother, Mrs. O'Neill, had a baby, it was a time to celebrate in their house. When Mindy's sister, Twila, talked about being pregnant, it was awful. What made the difference?

▸ Sometimes Christian kids think, *If I do something wrong, I'll just ask Jesus to protect me.* Does it work that way? Why or why not? How can someone's life be wrecked if they depend on God's protection when doing something wrong?

▸ After people sin, they often think or say, "God will never forgive me for what I've done." Yet if Twila asks God, He *will* forgive her. What words could Twila use to ask God's forgiveness?

▸ **When people are truly sorry and ask forgiveness, God always forgives their sin. Yet people still need to live with the consequences of sin.** What is a consequence?

▸ If Twila hadn't become pregnant, would there still be consequences for her sin? What are some possible consequences? In what ways will Twila's choices in life be limited? What are some things she might not be able to do?

▸ What choices will Twila need to make about her baby?

▸ If Twila has an abortion, what will happen to the baby? How do you feel about that? How do you think God feels about abortion? For a mega clue check out Exodus 20:13.

▸ Who is the one who gives life? How do you know that every life is valuable to Him?

Your eyes saw my unformed body. All the days ordained for me were written in your book before one of them came to be. Psalm 139:16

Thank you, God, that every life is created by you. Help me remember how much you value my life and the life of every person you create. Help me to keep the creation of new life as something holy and beautiful.

Shorty's Discovery

When the phone jangled, Adam was the one who picked it up.

"Hey, Shorty—"

There it was again. *Shorty.* Adam felt like not answering.

But the voice on the other end kept talking. "We've got a tournament going at the park. The Bears against the Tigers, and one of the guys on our team got sick—"

"Aw, Stretch," Adam interrupted without giving a thought to his friend's name. "You know I don't like playing volleyball."

"But hey, c'mon—help us out. The Bears are in a jam."

Adam and Stretch had been friends for years, but Adam kept thinking up excuses. Stretch wouldn't listen, and Adam was afraid to say what was really wrong.

How can I tell him I'm too short? I can't get the ball over the net. I can't spike 'em like he does. I'm just a big zero.

But Stretch didn't take no for an answer. "I'll drop by on the way to the park." Before Adam could answer, Stretch hung up.

Half an hour later, he pounded on the door. Adam still

didn't feel good about playing. This last year Stretch had shot up, and he was more than a head taller than Adam. To make matters worse, Adam was shorter than all the boys his age. He avoided every volleyball game he could.

"It'll be great to play with you again, Shorty," Stretch said on the way to the park.

Adam stopped dead in his tracks. His anger boiled up and spilled over. "I can't stand being called Shorty."

"Well, do you think I like being called Stretch?"

"That's different."

"No, it's not. Everywhere I go, people turn around and stare at me."

"You mean it's as awful being too tall as it is being too short?"

"You bet!"

"But it'd be great to be tall. You're better in sports. You beat out all the other kids."

When Stretch laughed, Adam felt uncomfortable. *Shouldn't have opened my big mouth.*

But when Stretch spoke, his voice was quiet. "I just don't fight it anymore."

"Fight it?"

"The way I am. I can't help that I'm tall, the same way you can't help being short. Why fight it?"

"What do you mean?"

"It's in the *genes*. My mom and dad are tall, and I'm tall. Your mom and dad are short, and you're short. It's like getting blue eyes or brown hair. So what's the big deal?"

Adam didn't have an answer for that. From science class he knew that the chromosomes he received from his mom and dad contained genes. Those genes decided how he'd look—the color of eyes and hair and skin, the shape of his hands and feet, and yes, his height.

Adam thought back to his family's reunion a month before. At least a hundred times someone had said, "Wow! You sure look like your dad!" Adam got tired of hearing about it, yet he had to admit he was glad he *did* look like Dad—except for being short, that is.

Soon Adam and Stretch reached the park, and Stretch started lining up the other Bears. "You stand next to me, Shorty."

"So you can get all the ones I miss?" Adam wanted to say.

But while the Tigers, the guys on the other team, found their places, Stretch leaned over and spoke in a soft voice. "Go for the fast ones. Set 'em up, and I'll spike 'em."

Big deal, thought Adam. *Way to make yourself look good.*

When the serve came his way, Adam tried to spike it himself. It headed straight for the center of the net.

Stretch didn't say anything, and the next chance he got, Adam tried again. Once more the ball headed into the net and dropped to the ground. The Tigers jumped ahead, 7 to 9.

This time Adam caught Stretch looking at him.

"Trying to help the other side?" Stretch asked.

Feeling uncomfortable, Adam turned away. *I've lost two points for us. Maybe Stretch is right. But why should I help him look good?"*

On the next serve, the ball dropped on the other side of Stretch. He started for it, but didn't move fast enough. The ball touched the ground, and the Tigers gained another point.

Stretch should've made that, Adam told himself. *If I'd been that close, I'd have had it.*

In that instant another thought flashed through Adam's mind. *There* is *something I can do better—I can move faster!*

It felt good to know that. In a quiet moment between serves, he thought about it. *We each have different abilities. So why am I trying to look better than Stretch?*

Adam straightened his shoulders and stood ready. "Okay, you old Tigers," he said under his breath. "Get out of our way!"

As the Bears started their serve, Adam and Stretch played close to the net. When the Tigers volleyed the ball back to them, Adam set it up. Stretch spiked it. Sure enough, the Bears got a point!

Before long, Adam knew that he and Stretch were a good team. When a quick move was needed, Adam went for it. More than once he set up the ball. But when they needed a leap or spike, Adam got out of the way, and Stretch took it. The game ended with the Bears winning, 15 to 13.

Stretch slapped Adam on the back. "How about playing again next week, Shorty?"

"Sounds good," Adam said. For once, he didn't mind his other name.

TO **TALK** ABOUT

▸ Stretch had learned something important about how to handle his height. What was it?

▸ Kids take growth spurts at different times, and boys often gain their height later than girls. But Adam might always be shorter than other boys. Why? How do genes affect a person's height?

▸ There are many other ways that genes affect the way you look and grow. What are some of them? You might like to check a children's encyclopedia. Try looking under *gene*, *genetics*, and *heredity*.

▸ What did Adam discover about Stretch's playing ability? What ability did Adam offer the team?

▸ What are some things you can't change about yourself? What does it mean to inherit certain traits? What good traits, or strengths, have you inherited?

▸ What are ways you can learn new skills or put your strengths to good use?

My frame was not hidden from you when I was made in the secret place. When I was woven together in the depths of the earth, your eyes saw my unformed body. Psalm 139:15–16a

Thank you, God, for the genes you gave me. Help me to be happy with the things about me that I can't change. Help me develop the strengths you've given me.

The Right Touch

"It's for you, Dad," said Nikki as she held out the phone.

Dad pulled himself out of his favorite chair. "Keep down the noise. I'll take it in the other room."

As Dad talked on the phone, Nikki looked around the circle that was her family. Mom sat next to a light, knitting a sweater. Amy played on the floor, dressing her favorite doll. In another corner Terry and Paul raced cars together. In that moment Nikki thought about how much all of them meant to her.

Dad returned with a wide grin on his face. "Guess what?" he asked.

"You're going out of town on business," said Paul.

"We're going to move again," Terry guessed.

Mom looked up and her gaze met Dad's. Whatever she saw there took the concerned look from her eyes.

"Keep trying," Dad told them.

"You have a meeting this weekend," Amy answered.

Dad shook his head. "No, no, no!"

"You're all guessing wrong," Nikki said. "The way Dad

looks, it must be something good. Oh, I know! You won the sales contest!"

"Right!" Dad's eyes shone. "I won the trip for two. Your mother and I could fly to Florida, stay in a hotel near the beach, go sight-seeing, and enjoy ourselves for a week."

"Good for you, Dad!" Nikki exclaimed.

But Dad held up his hands. "Wait a minute! I'm not through yet. Your mom and I had a vacation together four months ago. So I asked my boss if I could make a trade. What if I drove to Florida instead of flying? And what if I stayed in a less expensive hotel? Could I take all of you instead?"

"Really, Dad?" A chorus went up. "We can all go?"

Dad grinned and went into his deepest voice. "He said, 'Fine, Jennings, fine. I'm all for family vacations myself.'"

Everyone jumped up. Amy squealed. Paul took a flying leap and landed in Dad's arms. Terry followed. Suddenly the room filled with laughter and hugs.

What a good feeling it is to be a family, Nikki thought as she hugged Dad and Mom, Amy, and her brothers. *What a good feeling it is to love each other.*

The celebration continued around her, but in the next instant, Nikki's happiness dimmed. *Uncle Henry lives on the way to Florida. Are we going to see him again?*

Like a picture in Nikki's mind, she remembered the last time they visited him. Nikki tried to brush aside the memory, but she couldn't. She thought about Uncle Henry and how he tried to touch the private parts of her body. Even now, Nikki felt uncomfortable just thinking about it.

Why is it fun having my family hug me? Nikki asked herself. *And why is it awful when Uncle Henry tries?*

Quietly Nikki sat down next to Dad. Dad looked at her and asked, "What's the matter, Nikki?"

Should I tell him? Nikki debated within herself. *Should I say something about Uncle Henry? Or should I pretend everything is okay?*

Dad seemed to read her face. "If there's something wrong, telling me can make a difference."

Is that really true? Nikki wondered. *Would Dad make a difference?*

Nikki hesitated, thinking things over. *What if he doesn't believe me?*

A moment later everyone but Dad scattered to other parts of the house. Nikki sat on the floor, still thinking. Finally she decided to give it a try.

"When we go on the trip, will we see Uncle Henry again?"

"Probably," Dad said. "Why?"

"He makes me feel creepy," answered Nikki.

"What do you mean?" Dad asked.

"He made me promise I wouldn't tell anyone."

"Then I think it's important that you tell me. Sometimes when adults tell you not to say anything, it's because something is wrong. That's different from being a tattletale—someone who tells stories about another kid to make trouble."

"You know, that's just how it felt," Nikki said slowly. "Like something was wrong. It didn't feel good. Last summer, when we were alone once, Uncle Henry touched me in private places."

A flash of anger crossed Dad's face, an anger that Nikki knew was for Uncle Henry, not for her.

"I'm glad you told me," Dad said. "Your body is very special, and it belongs to you. Uncle Henry shouldn't touch you that way. Your mother and I will make sure it doesn't happen again."

"But what should I do if he tries?"

"We won't give him the chance. We won't see Uncle Henry on the way to Florida. But if someone else ever tries something like that, you can say, 'NO!' in the biggest voice you have. You can say, 'I don't want to be touched that way.' Get away from that person and tell Mom or me at once."

Nikki stood up, but Dad wasn't finished yet. "I'm glad you told me what happened, Nikki. But if you ever have trouble with anyone, tell Mom or me right away. I promise you, it won't happen again."

Already Nikki felt better. When Dad hugged her, it was a healing kind of touch. Nikki felt as if a bag filled with stones had rolled off her back. Telling Dad really *did* make a difference.

TO TALK ABOUT

▸ Why is it important that Nikki told her dad about the way Uncle Henry treated her?

▸ If her dad hadn't believed what Nikki said, what other adults could she talk with? Think of people Nikki would know from her family, church, or school.

▸ **Good touch makes kids feel loved, happy, and peaceful inside themselves.** What are some times when you've enjoyed being hugged by your family, relatives, or friends? How did you feel afterward?

▸ **Bad touch makes kids feel confused, sad, ashamed, or scared.** Bad touch may involve the parts of your body covered by your swimsuit. What can you tell a person who touches you in a way you don't like?

▸ What if someone offered you some money or candy and then tried to do something that makes you uncomfortable? Do you think that would be good touch or bad touch? Why?

▸ **If you feel uncomfortable about the way a person touches you, you always have the right to tell someone about it.** How can the right adult change what is happening?

▸ Pretend you're out in a park and someone with a neat dog comes by. You don't know the owner, but the man or woman says you can take the dog for a walk. Would you do it? Why or why not?

▸ Or you're walking home from school and someone you don't know stops his car and calls out the window, "I lost my puppy. Will you help me find it?" Would you walk over to the car? Would you help that person find the puppy? Why or why not?

▸ It's important for you to obey adults when they ask you to do something. But it's different if an adult asks you to do something wrong. Then you should say NO! or run away, and then ask the right person for help. The Bible tells us about Daniel and what he did when evil people tried to force him to do something wrong. See Daniel 6:1–

10. Why do you think the men were mean to Daniel? Did Daniel allow them to win, or did he try to change what was happening? How do you know?

▶ What miracle did God give Daniel? Read Daniel 6:11–23. Why do people say, "Dare to be a Daniel"?

For the eyes of the Lord range throughout the earth to strengthen those whose hearts are fully committed to him.
2 Chronicles 16:9a

Thank you, Jesus, for all the times I've felt your love because my family and friends hug me in the right way. If I'm ever uncomfortable with the way people touch me, help me to say NO! and talk to the right grown-up. Thank you that talking to the right person will make a difference in what happens to me.

A Message
for Michael

When the note came to his desk, Michael felt a tingle of dread. This had happened before, right after Dad became manager of a restaurant in town. Folded small, wrinkled and dirty, the note looked as if it had passed through many hands. His name was printed in big letters.

As he glanced up, Mike saw kids watching him. *They'll wait till I open it,* he thought.

A minute later the teacher left the room, and Mike unfolded the note. It was for him, all right.

"To Michael," it began. As he read the words, he felt the hot flush of embarrassment reach his face.

On one side was a cartoon showing how Mike looked when he walked across the stage at the fall concert. Because teachers knew that he was especially gifted, they had asked him to play a piano solo between the band and choir numbers.

The note described Mike and his toothpick legs: *"You look like a skinny girl. You're stupid and you're a sissy.*

Only girls play the piano. You don't have a friend in the whole world."

Worst of all were the kind of words sprinkled between the mean thoughts. Mike wasn't sure what some of the words meant, but the few he did know told him too much. From the top of his head right down to his toes, he felt upset.

Wish I could crawl in a hole, Mike thought. He wanted to shout, "I hate you!"

Just in time, he remembered that whoever wrote the mean words was probably watching. Mike slipped the note into his jeans pocket and tried not to show how he felt. Just the same, the words burned into his mind.

In the next two days, Mike tried to act as if nothing had happened. Yet now and then, when he was by himself, he took out the note and read it. It took a while before he realized that the note had four or five different kinds of handwriting. *Did they pass around the paper? It looks like each kid added something.*

From then on, whenever Mike looked at someone in his classroom, he wondered, *Are you one of them? Did you write that note?*

The more Mike thought about the words, the more he dreaded going back to school each day. Most of all, he dreaded playing the piano at the spring concert. It was only one week away.

A month before, he had finished memorizing the piece he planned to play—Prelude in C-sharp Minor, by Rachmaninoff [Rahk-MAHN-ih-nawf]. Every day since, he had played the prelude almost without a mistake. But suddenly, as he practiced one evening, Mike couldn't remember the music. His mind went blank except for two thoughts: *They think I look like a girl. They think I'm a sissy.*

Then Mike remembered the rest of the note. *I'm stupid, just like they said. I don't have a friend in the world. How can I ever play the piano in front of the whole school?*

In that moment everything seemed impossible. Mike's hands crashed down on the keys. Without moving, he sat hunched over, staring at the keyboard.

His dad found Mike there. "Hey, what's the matter?"

"Nothing," Mike answered, unwilling to look at Dad's face.

But Mom joined them. "That's not true. I can tell by the way you're playing. What's wrong?"

Looking up, Mike searched Dad's face, then Mom's. Finally Mike dug into his jeans pocket. Without a word he handed the note to Dad.

"I see," Dad said after reading the note. He handed it to Mom.

As she read, her face crumpled. "Oh, Mike, that's awful! How long have you had this?"

"Since Monday."

Mom blinked away the tears on her lashes. "And you didn't tell us? How did it make you feel?"

For a long moment Mike couldn't speak. When he did, his voice was low. "Well, I sure have toothpick legs. So maybe they're right. Maybe I *am* stupid! Am I a sissy because I play the piano?"

"Oh no!" Dad said. "Of course you're not a sissy!"

But Mike's frustration and anger tumbled out. "Why me?

What did I do to make the kids pick on me?"

Dad read the note again. "Maybe it's not you they're picking on. Last weekend I had to ask five or six boys your age to stop hanging around the restaurant. When one of them swore at me, I told him that his language wasn't acceptable."

Dad looked thoughtful. "If that's what happened, I'm sorry they took it out on you. *Really* sorry. I was right in what I did, but I'm sorry for you."

"It happened once before," Mike said. "I was afraid to tell you."

"Hey," Dad said. "You can always talk to us. We're all in this together. We love you, remember?"

Mike nodded. "But there's something that scares me. Do you think I'll get another note after the concert?"

"If you do, let me read it first," Dad said.

As Mom and Dad talked with Mike, a new thought dropped into his mind. "Most of the great piano players have been men. I wonder if they all got picked on?"

Dad laughed. "Well, whether you're a boy or a girl, you'll never be able to please everyone. Just because a kid says something, it doesn't mean that it's true."

Turning back to the piano, Mike started playing again. As soon as he thought about the mean boys, his fingers felt clumsy. When he missed one note after another, Mike stopped.

"The concert is only a week away!" His voice rose. "How can I possibly play in front of those kids?"

At first Dad was silent, thinking. Then he said, "You

know, when someone hurts you, there's only one thing to do."

"What's that?"

"Forgive them."

"But how?" Mike felt even more angry. "I wanna hate those kids! If I forgive 'em, it's like saying that what they did was okay!"

"Not on your life!" Dad exclaimed. "What they did was wrong. If you forgive them, it's because that's what Jesus would do. Remember how He promised to forgive us as we forgive others?"

When Mike nodded, Dad went on. "Forgiving someone who hurts you gives you a way to stop hurting. You start feeling better."

Mike wasn't sure he believed Dad. But then Mike thought about the concert and how his fingers wouldn't move. "I don't have any choice, do I?"

"Not really."

"Okay," Mike mumbled. With his eyes wide open, he said a quick prayer. "Jesus, in your name I forgive those kids."

When he finished, Mike felt no different. He wondered if he really meant what he prayed. Maybe sometime it would seem that he did.

Then he thought about all the times he had read the cruel words. Taking the note from Dad, Mike tore the paper into tiny bits. When he tossed them into a wastebasket, he was surprised to discover what a relief it was.

On the day of the concert, Mike felt like hot oil skittering around a frying pan. Each time he looked at the kids, his hurt started to come back.

Then Mike remembered tearing up the note. *I've forgiven them. I don't want to think about it again!*

In that moment something changed inside Mike. Again he felt surprised. He didn't hate the kids anymore. As he formed a plan in his mind, he knew exactly what to do.

When Mike walked out on the stage that night, he felt more scared than he'd ever been in his life. But more than anything, he didn't want the kids to know how nervous he felt.

Crossing the stage, Mike reached the piano bench. When he sat down, he turned to the audience. At first it seemed a blur, a wilderness of faces. Then he saw Mom and Dad.

Mike's lips felt stiff, but he smiled. Mom smiled back, and Dad looked like he wanted to clap.

Then Mike faced the piano again. *Jesus,* he thought. The name was a prayer.

In that moment Mike felt a sureness flow through him. As he held his hands above the keyboard, they grew steady.

Mike struck the opening octaves of Prelude in C-sharp Minor. As his fingers sank into the chords, the auditorium grew still.

Mike forgot about the kids who listened. He forgot about the words they'd written. He just felt the music. Its fire raced through his fingers. Every note fell clean and sure.

When the applause broke around him, Mike stood and took his bows. To his amazement people in the front row stood up. Then like a wave in the sea, one person after another rose in a standing ovation. The boys from his class had no choice but to rise with them.

Once again Mike smiled. This time his smile was real.

TO **TALK** ABOUT

▸ When kids made fun of how Mike looked, how did he feel about his body? About his ability to play the piano?

▸ The kids may have sent Mike the note because of what happened at the restaurant, or they might have just decided to pick on him. Do you think any of the boys felt jealous of Mike and his ability? Explain.

▸ What did Mike do to work out his problem? Why is it important that he talked with his mom and dad about the note?

▸ When Mike forgave the kids, did it mean that what they did was right? Explain why you think the way you do.

▸ What if Mike *hadn't* torn up the note? Do you think his feelings about it would get worse or better? Why? Give reasons for your answer.

▸ Suppose that Mike *didn't* receive a standing ovation. Would he have won anyway? Why or why not?

▸ Has anyone ever said something mean about your physical appearance? How did it make you feel? What did you do about it?

▸ If you'd like to walk in the footprints of Jesus, here are some steps you can take:
  • Talk about the mean thing that happened to you with someone who understands.
  • Know something big: **If you forgive someone, it doesn't mean that what the person did is right.**
  • **Choose to forgive the person who was mean to**

you. Pray in the strong name of Jesus: "In your name, Jesus, I forgive that person."

- Ask Jesus to clean out your hurt feelings. Think about good words, such as a Bible verse. Keep repeating that verse to yourself until you feel peaceful inside.
- Leave what happened behind you. Don't keep going back to wade in the mud puddle. Jesus asked us to pray, "Forgive us our sins as we forgive others." Keep thinking about Jesus and his words.

[Jesus said,] "Blessed are you when people insult you, persecute you and falsely say all kinds of evil against you because of me. Rejoice and be glad, because great is your reward in heaven." Matthew 5:11-12a

Jesus, it really hurts when someone is mean to me. Yet when people were mean to you, you forgave them. You even forgave them when they nailed you to the cross! Because of that, Jesus, I forgive the kids who hurt me. Heal me, so their words don't hurt me anymore. Thank you!

At Home
Next Door

Without making a sound, Darcy closed the back door behind her. Like a shadow she crept down the steps, then through the yard. A moment later she knocked on her neighbor's back door.

To her relief Shannon was the one who answered. "Hi, there! C'mon in. Haven't seen you for a while."

Darcy said, "Hi, yourself," then felt shy. But Shannon made her feel welcome.

"I've missed you. Remember how we used to talk about stuff?"

Feeling miserable inside, Darcy nodded. Now that she was here, she didn't know where to begin. Again Shannon filled in the gaps.

"I just made some of your favorite cookies."

As Darcy sat down at the kitchen table, it seemed like old times. Shannon was eighteen and had always seemed like an older sister to Darcy. Whenever things got too hard at home, Darcy escaped and came here.

Shannon knew that. "What's the matter?" she asked after the third cookie.

"I just—" Darcy felt too old to cry, but tears spilled down her cheeks.

"Your mom and dad fighting again?"

Darcy nodded.

"How are you feeling about it?"

Darcy thought for a moment. "I'm not scared the way I was when I was a little kid. Then I wondered if one of them would hurt me. Beat me up, I mean. They never have, but—"

Darcy stopped, trying to think it through. "Now I get scared in other ways. Boys at school notice me, and sometimes I like them."

Shannon waited, so Darcy had to go on. "But what if. . . ?"

"What if what?"

Darcy didn't smile. "What if they treat me the way my dad treats my mom?"

"That's a good question."

Darcy leaned forward. "Shannon, when I see your mom and dad, they have a good time together. They act like they *love* each other."

"They do," Shannon said. "Every now and then they disagree about something, but they talk it out. They *do* love each other."

"And when I come over here, it's different." Darcy looked down at the kitchen floor. She was afraid to tell Shannon how miserable she really felt.

Just the same, Shannon guessed. "Darcy, are you wondering about this because when you grow up, you want to be happy like my mom and dad?"

"Sounds kind of dumb, huh? Thinking about it now?"

"Sounds kind of smart to me."

"For you it's easy," Darcy said. "You've watched your mom and dad all your life. You can try to be like them. But what about me?"

"You're right." Shannon's green eyes were deep and serious. "It probably *will* be easier for me. But you can learn from my mom and dad, too. Pick out what you like about the way they live. They aren't perfect any more than anyone else. But try to remember what you like."

"But—" Darcy didn't know how to say it. She tried again. "Why do your mom and dad have it so good, and my mom and dad have it so awful?"

Shannon thought for a moment. "Well, the most important thing is that they're both Christians. That doesn't always mean a marriage is good, but it helps. Mom and Dad pray together, and when they disagree about something, they ask Jesus to help them know what to do."

"How did they find each other?"

Shannon grinned. "When I was a little kid, I thought this was so romantic. But now I think it's something really important. When my mom was still a young girl, her mom—my grandma—taught her to pray about who she'd marry. And my dad's dad—my grandpa—taught him to pray about who *he'd* marry!"

"How did they know what to look for?"

Again Shannon grinned. "Well, I can tell you *that*. Or I'll tell you what *I'm* looking for!

"Mom says the kind of marriage I'll have depends a lot

on the kind of choices I make. For both boys and girls, it's important to know what they want *before* they start getting serious about someone."

Shannon stood up, poured Darcy some milk, and sat down again. "First of all, I want to marry a Christian. Someone who feels as strongly about being a Christian as I do. Some girls marry a guy who goes to church, but if both of them aren't really committed to the Lord, they still wind up having a problem."

For a moment Shannon was quiet. "And I want someone who respects me."

"What do you mean?"

"Well, some boys take a girl on a date to see what they can get away with. They try to take girls to a lonely place and park. So don't let yourself get stuck in a lonely place. Or don't invite a boy over when your mom and dad are working. Sometimes girls think, 'I'll lose my boyfriend if I don't do what he wants.' Instead, that's the surest way to lose him."

Darcy thought about that. She felt scared to ask, to be that honest with anyone. But then the words tumbled out. "A health ed. teacher talking about sex made me feel I was strange for wanting to wait until I got married. Is it *really* okay to say no?"

"You bet it's okay to say no! That's being good to yourself. It's okay to say, 'I don't want to be pushed.' It's okay to have ideals."

"Ideals?"

"To wait with sex until marriage," Shannon told her. "You know, I heard a speaker I trust talk about sex. He said studies show that people who wait have a better chance of being happy within a marriage."

"But what if a boy really loves me?"

"Oh, lots of boys will say they love you. And they'll say to you, 'If you love me, prove it.' "

"Prove it?"

"Yeah, that's the line they use to get girls to go further sexually than a girl wants to go," Shannon said. "That's where a lot of girls get stuck with someone who's wrong for them."

"But you're sure someone like that wouldn't really love me?"

"Not on your life. If someone really loves you, he cares about what happens to you. He wouldn't purposely do something to hurt you."

Shannon leaned forward. "You want to be able to do the things you really want to do. Like graduating from high school. Like getting trained for a job or going to college. You want to wait for a husband you *really* love. If a guy doesn't respect you, he'll make you lose respect for yourself. And self-respect is one of the most important things you have."

For a moment Shannon was quiet. "There's something more."

"What's that?" Darcy asked.

"Saying no to sex outside of marriage is living God's way. It's dreaming big. It's letting God help you become all He wants you to be."

For a moment the kitchen was quiet. Then Darcy thought of another question. "How will I know if I really love someone?"

"He'll be someone you think a lot of." Shannon's ideas

tumbled out. "You'll respect him and like the way he acts. You should be able to talk with him, even about hard things. You have fun together, even though you don't spend big money doing it. You miss him when he's gone, and you like doing nice things for him."

"And he's good-lookin' . . ."

Shannon grinned. "Of course!" Then her eyes turned serious. "But Mom says that when you love someone, no matter how that person looks, he seems good-looking."

"What about love at first sight?"

Shannon laughed. "You've really been thinking about this. Well, from what my mom says—"

A voice interrupted. "And what does your mom say?"

Darcy looked up, glad to see Shannon's mom, but wishing she hadn't come now.

"My mom-m-m says," Shannon drawled, "there's a difference between being attracted to a boy and really loving him. You can like the way a boy looks at first sight. But love is more."

Shannon and her mom said together, "Love grows."

"You need to give it time so you know for sure," said Shannon's mom.

Darcy stood up. "Gotta go now. Thanks for the cookies."

Shannon went to the door with Darcy and gave her a hug. "Come over again soon, okay?"

Darcy nodded, knowing she'd be back. "Thanks, Shannon," she said softly. Then she bounded across the yard and slipped through the back door. As she tiptoed up the stairs to her room, the house was quiet. Mom and Dad had stopped fighting. Until the next time.

As Darcy crawled into bed, she prayed for them. Then, for the first time, she prayed about who she might someday marry.

TO **TALK** ABOUT

▸ Why is it helpful to spend a lot of time in groups of kids before you get serious with one person?

▸ What are some of the qualities you want to find in the people you choose for your closest friends? How can you learn to recognize those qualities when you're in a group of kids your age?

▸ Why is it important to know how you want to handle yourself *before* you start a serious relationship with one person?

▸ ***Both* boys and girls need to be responsible in the way they act.** In what ways can a boy respect a girl and be thoughtful about what's best for her? How can a girl be thoughtful and responsible in the way she treats a boy?

▸ Galatians 5:22–25 says something important about self-control. What *is* self-control? What are some ways to show self-control?

▸ Sometimes young people believe they're in love and later discover it was just infatuation—a liking for someone that doesn't last. How would you feel if you got too involved physically with a boy or girl, then discovered you didn't "love" that person anymore?

▸ The Bible tells us that sexual intercourse outside marriage is a sin against our bodies. Yet within marriage, intercourse is beautiful and God's way for a man and woman to express love to one another. How can the way a person acts sexually be a matter of obedience to God? (Obedience is responding to what God likes, not because we have to, but because we love Him.)

▶ See 1 Corinthians 6:18–20. What does it mean to be a temple of the Holy Spirit? What does it mean to honor God with your body?

▶ If you are old enough and have the blessing of your family, growing in a relationship with a person you love and plan to marry can be exciting and fun. But some relationships offer only misery. What do you think makes the difference?

▶ What are some ways to know if love is real? Some clues are in the story. For more ideas take a look at 1 Corinthians 13.

▶ Whether you're a boy or girl, why is it important to pray about who you might someday marry?

Do you not know that your body is a temple of the Holy Spirit, who is in you, whom you have received from God? You are not your own; you were bought at a price. Therefore honor God with your body. 1 Corinthians 6:19–20

Thank you, Jesus, that I can learn a lot about other kids by having fun in a group. Help me to recognize the qualities that are important in my special friends. If you want me to get married someday, I ask in your name to give me someone with those good qualities. I want to marry the Christian who is your choice for me.

The Day of
the Storm

As Peter sat at the supper table, he stretched out his leg. Suddenly he kicked his sister, Pam.

"Stop it!" she exclaimed, glaring at her twin.

Pete's leg was already back under his chair. He looked as innocent as a newborn baby.

Mom sighed. "What's the matter with you two? All day long—fight, fight, fight."

Dad put down his fork and looked up. "Leave your sister alone, Pete. As long as you're done eating, you can start the dishes."

"Dishes? That's girl's work!"

"Girl's work?" asked Dad.

"Yeah, girl's work! You don't really expect me to do the dishes, do you?"

"Yes, I do. That's why I asked."

"But only girls do dishes. That's Pamela's job."

"You just don't wanna do 'em," she growled.

Mom looked at Pam, then at Pete. "I think she's right, Pete."

Groaning, he stood up. With every dish he carried to the sink, he had a new complaint. Finally Dad said, "No more comments, Pete, okay?"

"Yeah, Peterrrr!" Pam drawled.

Mom looked at Dad and rolled her eyes. Clearly she was tired of their arguments.

Dad looked thoughtful. "Pam, I'd like to have you mow the lawn."

"Dad! You've gotta be kidding. *Me* mow the lawn?"

"Yes, *you* mow the lawn," answered Dad. "It's going to rain soon, so get started right away."

"But what if someone sees me? I'd be so embarrassed doing my brother's work!"

Dad grinned. "Oh? His work? You're sure?"

"I'm sure! I don't wanna get all hot and sweaty!"

"Hey, I'll trade with you, Pam," Pete said quickly.

Dad winked at Mom. "Nope, no trades. Not tonight. I think we should do a bit of thinking about male and female roles around here."

"Oh, Da-a-a-a-d!" the twins groaned, together for a change.

"I mean it!" Dad said. "Is there such a thing as boy's work and girl's work? Or can we all just pitch in when something needs to be done?"

Mom smiled, but neither Pam nor Pete seemed to like Dad's idea.

"I haven't thought much about it before," he said. "But maybe your mom and I have taught you to fill certain roles just by the way we treat you. Is that good or bad or somewhere in between?"

Pete jumped on it. "That's good! Look at the name you gave me. I'm a rock!" He flexed the muscles in his arms. "Strength, power, everything you want!"

Then Pete had an idea. As he picked up another plate, he let his voice sound only half interested. "What does Pam's name mean, anyway?"

"Loving, kind," answered Mom, falling into the trap. "All honey."

"All honey!" Pete hooted. "She's all honey, all right!"

Pam's eyes glistened with anger. "I don't know why I have to have you for a brother! And a *twin* brother at that!"

Dad's grin faded. "Okay, that's enough. Both of you get to work." He stood up. For a moment he peered toward the trees in the backyard. "Seems like it's getting dark faster than usual. Get the mowing done right away, Pam." Dad picked up his paper and went into the living room.

As Pete washed the dishes, he stared out the kitchen window. Before long he noticed dark clouds moving in. Through the open window he sensed the stillness. Not a leaf on the nearby maple moved.

Soon the clouds were directly overhead. Watching Pam take slow turns around the yard, Pete felt uneasy. He was still scrubbing pans when the sky changed to an eerie green.

Pam had only half of the lawn mowed when the wind came up, whipping through the trees.

Pete left the dishes and headed for the backyard. "Hey, Pam! Run for it!"

Grabbing the handle of the mower, he raced for the garage. The moment he pushed the mower inside, he slammed down the door and followed Pam.

Near the house, the rising wind pushed him against the wall. A strong gust ripped through a nearby maple, and Pete heard a crack. A large limb landed on the lawn.

Dad met him at the door. "Head for the basement!"

With a bound Pete reached the steps, and he took them two at a time. Partway down, he twisted his ankle and tumbled the rest of the way.

When he landed at the bottom of the steps, Pete moaned. Clutching his ankle, he rolled on the floor. "Ow, ow, ow!"

Their eyes full of concern, Mom, Dad, and Pam knelt around him.

"Did you hit your head?" Mom asked.

"Oh, Pete, I'm sorry," Pam said. "It's 'cause you were helping me."

"It's 'cause I was doing girl's work," Pete growled. "If I'd been mowing the lawn, I'd have been done!"

As he tried to sit up, he moved his leg and winced. "Owww!" Lying back down again, Pete groaned.

"Just lie still for a minute," Dad said.

"Did you feel anything snap?" asked Mom.

Pete shook his head.

"Can you move your foot?" Dad asked.

As Pete tried to move his leg, he winced. The pain brought tears to his eyes.

"Boys aren't supposed to cry," said Pam sweetly, sounding like her old self.

Suddenly Dad and Mom laughed.

"I don't see what's funny," Pete grumbled. "I'm lying here dying, and you're all laughing."

Just then the lights flickered and went out. In the darkness Pete heard Mom laugh again, but this time there was a nervous sound in her voice.

"Take it easy, honey," Dad told her. "Where's the flashlight that's supposed to be down here?"

"On the shelf," Pam said. "Just a sec. I'll get it."

In a minute she turned on the flashlight. Then she lit the candles they kept in the basement.

Dad turned on the battery-operated radio. "Straight-line winds have left a path of destruction through the center part of the state. . . ."

Mom was still on the floor next to Pete. "I think it's a sprain."

Dad slid a pillow under Pete's head and slipped off his shoe. Gathered around him, the family waited in the basement until sounds of the storm moved farther away. At last the thunder rumbled off in the distance.

"The brunt of the storm has now left the metro area," the newscaster told them. "Cleanup crews are clearing the main roads. Go out only if necessary. Remember that any electric lines that are down may be live."

"We better take you in to urgent care," Dad told Pete.

He and Mom helped Pete up the steps and into the car. As soon as Pam jumped in, Dad backed out of the driveway. He drove slowly, weaving around the branches in the road. "Good thing we have only six blocks to go."

But for Pete it seemed like sixty miles. Staring out the

157

window, he tried not to move his ankle. It hurt more every minute.

Around them, chain saws roared as crews tried to clear fallen branches. An electric company van blocked one street as three people worked on a power line.

When Dad stopped the car, Pam pointed up at a post. "See that woman? She's working with 'em!"

"Hush!" Mom said. "Leave Pete alone!"

Dad turned the car, but two blocks away they ran into trouble again. The signal lights were off, and the few cars that were out moved slowly. Someone in a yellow rain coat waved them around another fallen tree. Pete didn't need Pam's help to see that the police officer was a woman.

At the hospital, Pam stayed in the waiting room, and Mom and Dad helped Pete into the emergency room. Before long, a man dressed in a white shirt and pants appeared. As he started asking questions, Pete had a question for him. "Are you the doctor?"

"Nope, I'm a nurse. Let's see what you've got here." Gently he pulled down Pete's sock. "Now, this is going to be a bit uncomfortable, but I need to take off your sock before there's any more swelling."

When Pete left the hospital, Mom was on one side, Dad on the other. Pam trailed behind. The doctor said it was a bad sprain. Pete would have to use crutches and stay off his ankle for a while.

In the days that followed, Pete took full advantage of the doctor's orders. Whenever he could, he ordered Pam around. But often he thought about all that had happened the day of the storm. He started watching how Dad handled certain things.

"Here, let me get that," Dad told Mom one day when she brought home heavy bags of salt for the softener.

Another time Dad said, "Praying isn't a sign of weakness." After that, Pete noticed how often Dad prayed, when it seemed he was just sitting in his chair.

On a night when Mom was really tired, Pete caught Dad doing the dishes. At one time Pete would have said, "That's sissy stuff!" Instead, he asked Dad, "You're making things easier for Mom, aren't you?" It wasn't really a question. Pete knew the answer.

Dad smiled. "When you were a baby, your mom worked extra long hours because I couldn't get a job. I changed your diapers. I did the dishes. I did all the things your mom would have done if she had been home. I love and respect your mother and want to help her."

As Dad let the water out of the sink, he winked. "And sometimes, in the middle of winter, she helps me shovel snow."

Lying in bed that night, Pete remembered Dad's words. "I'm glad I'm a boy," he told himself. "I *like* being what I am."

He would never ask Pam how she felt about being a girl. Pete thought he knew what she'd say.

But then, to his own surprise, Pete had another thought. *I wonder how God wants me to use my life serving Him?*

TO **TALK** ABOUT

▸ Pete said that doing dishes is girl's work. What do you think he's really saying?

▸ Pam said, "Boys aren't supposed to cry." What do you think she's really saying? Can you remember a time when Jesus cried? For a big clue see John 11:35. Why is it important that both boys and girls feel free to cry when needed?

▸ As a man and a woman, Pete's dad and mom have God-given differences. Yet that doesn't divide them. Instead, the differences in the way they were made help them work together. They seem happy in their male and female roles. What qualities make Pete's dad a special person? What qualities make Pete's mom a special person?

▸ Ideas keep changing about who does what kind of work. **What's really important is whether we are willing to help others and work together. When we care about others, we want the best for them, the way Jesus does.** What happened as long as Pete made himself number one? Was he happy? Why or why not? Give reasons for your answer.

▸ What happened as long as Pam kept teasing Pete? Do you think she was happy? Why or why not?

▸ In The Living Bible 1 Corinthians 13:5 reads, "Love does not demand its own way." What does that mean?

▸ A role model is someone who helps you know what kind of person you want to be. A role model acts in a way you'd like to act, or does things you'd like to do. If you're a girl, why is it important that you *like* being a girl? What women in the Bible would you like to be like?

▸ If you're a boy, why is it important that you *like* being a boy? What men in the Bible would you like to be like?

▸ Whether you're a boy or a girl, who is the very best role model you can have? Why?

Love is patient, love is kind. It does not envy, it does not boast, it is not proud. It is not rude, it is not self-seeking, it is not easily angered, it keeps no record of wrongs. 1 Corinthians 13:4-5

Lord, I like being who I am. Thank you that I live at a time when I'm free to try many different kinds of work. Help me to value the good things about being a boy and the good things about being a girl. Help me to use my life in serving you.

You Are Wonderfully Made!

While reading this book, you met a number of story kids who might be like someone you know. You learned about their choices. You probably made choices of your own. As time goes on, you'll be making more of them.

Perhaps you discovered that many small decisions add up to big ones. That's how you choose the side you want to be on—the side that values your body as something special.

That's also God's side. He values you. He values you exactly the way you are. But when you think about choosing His side, you may tell yourself, "I want to make good choices, but I don't know if I can."

Feeling helpless can be an okay place to be. In those scary moments, you have the biggest opportunity of all. That's when you can ask, "God, what do *you* want me to do? How do *you* want me to live?" Wherever you are, whatever you're doing, you can pray, "Help me, Jesus."

If you ask Him, Jesus *will* give you His help and the power of His Holy Spirit. But you also need to do your part by making good choices and following through.

When you receive help from the Holy Spirit, it doesn't mean that life will always be easy. Life wasn't easy for Jesus, either. That's why He understands how you feel. He knows about every one of your problems. He loves you so much that He died on the cross for you. And He promised to always be with you—no matter what you face.

Sometimes you may think it's hard to follow Jesus. If you need to say no to a temptation, you might wonder, "Is it worth it?" But when you *do* say no, you can look back later and think, "Whew! I'm glad I made that choice!" When you think about places where you could have fallen into deep, squishy mud, you'll be able to say, "Thank you, Jesus! You helped me escape that!"

As you look ahead, you'll discover something. **Every time you make a good choice, you make a footprint in the direction you want to go for your life.**

That's the miracle of dreaming big. That's having ideals and sticking to them. That's wanting with all your heart to follow in the footsteps of Jesus.

The God of miracles created you. His promise is forever: *"I made you and will care for you; I will give you help and rescue you"* (Isaiah 46:4b, TEV).

It's your life. The choices are up to you. But there's Someone always ready to help. His name is *Jesus*.

Acknowledgments

My gratitude to the Lord,
who gave me life and breath and made me all that I am.

To every person who has prayed for my writing
and to each of the following:

My husband, Roy,
for his ideas, love for children, and daily caring

Jeanne Szarzynski, physician assistant,
for reading the manuscript

Chuck Peterson, Betty Coleman,
Elaine Roub, Maude Dahlberg,
Cynthia Johnson, Leland Evenson, James Walfrid,
Kevin and Lyn Johnson,
Charette Barta, Penny Stokes,
Jerry Foley, and Terry White

Rochelle Glöege, Natasha Sperling,
and the entire Bethany team

As a writer, I value the person who changes the way I work
by offering encouragement, insight, and gracious honesty.
While editing the first edition of this series,
Traci Mullins
was that gift to me.

Word List

abdomen (AB-doe-men) stomach

abortion (uh-BOR-shun) removal of an unborn baby from the womb in such a way that it doesn't survive

acne (AK-nee) blackheads and pimples on the face and other parts of the body; often called "zits"

AIDS a disease caused by the HIV virus (VI-rus); the Human Immunodeficiency Virus destroys the body's ability to fight off illness; the letters in AIDS stand for Acquired Immune Deficiency Syndrome

amniotic sac (AM-nee-ot-ik sak) a bag full of liquid that protects the developing baby; also called bag of waters

anus (A-nus) opening through which solid waste passes out of the body

cervix (SUR-viks) opening between the uterus and the vagina

chromosome (CROW-muh-sohm) tiny threadlike particles that contain the genes received from both parents

circumcision (sur-come-SIZH-un) a minor operation that removes the loose fold of skin on a penis

clitoris (KLIT-o-ris) small, sensitive organ located just above a girl's urethra

conception (con-SEP-shun) when a sperm cell and an egg cell unite and God begins a new life

egg female sex cell; also called ovum (OH-vum)

embryo (EM-bree-oh) the new creation that forms after a sperm fertilizes the egg and conception occurs

erection (ih-REK-shun) when the penis becomes firm and stands out from the body

estrogen (ESS-tro-jen) hormones that cause the growth and development of female sexual characteristics; also influences the female reproductive system

Fallopian (fa-LOH-pee-an) **tubes** passageways that receive the female sex cell on its way to the uterus

fertilization (fur-til-eye-ZAY-shun) the genetic center of the sperm unites with the genetic center of the egg to create the beginning of a baby

fraternal (fra-TUR-nal) **twins** two sperm fertilize two eggs, and two babies are born at the same birth; may be the same sex, or one a girl and the other a boy

gene (jean) carries the hereditary traits that children receive from their parents

genitals (JEN-ah-tals) the external sex organs of boys or girls

homosexuality (ho-mo-sek-shoo-AL-ah-tee) sexual relationship between two people of the same sex

hormone (HOR-moan) starts the development of sexual traits in a boy or a girl

identical (i-DEN-ti-kal) **twins** a single fertilized egg grows into two babies instead of one; they will be of the same sex, born at the same birth, and very similar in appearance

immune (ih-MUNE) **system** parts of the body that work together to fight against sickness

labia (LAY-bee-ah) the soft lips surrounding the vagina and the outside of a girl's sexual organs

menstruation (men-stroo-AY-shun) release of tissue, egg, and waste blood from a girl's uterus, occurring about every twenty-eight days; also called a "period"

nutrient (NEW-tree-ent) the nourishment received from food

ovary (OH-va-ree) female reproductive organ that contains thousands of tiny eggs

ovulation (ah-view-LAY-shun) time when an ovary releases an egg; usually occurs monthly

pituitary (pi-TOO-ah-tare-ee) **gland** master gland of the body, which sends messages to other glands about growth and bodily functions

placenta (plah-CEN-tah) an organ that develops along with a growing baby during pregnancy and provides nourishment and oxygen for the baby

pornography (por-NOG-rah-fee) words and pictures that make sex dirty

puberty (PEW-bur-tee) the time at which a girl or boy becomes physically able to reproduce life

pubic (PEW-bik) the lowest part of the abdomen

sanitary (SAN-ah-tare-ee) **napkin** pad that absorbs menstrual flow and protects clothing during a girl's monthly period

scrotum (SKRO-tum) small bag of skin that holds the testicles; behind the penis

semen (SEE-men) combination of milky liquid and sperm produced by boys

sexual intercourse (SEX-shoo-al IN-ter-korse) a man's penis becomes firm and fits into a woman's vagina

sperm (spurm) male sex cell

tampon (TAM-pon) small roll of absorbent material inserted into a vagina to absorb mestrual flow

testicles (TES-ti-kuls) two male reproductive glands that produce sperm and testosterone

testosterone (tes-TOSS-tur-own) hormone that stimulates male sexual development and helps in production of sperm

umbilical (um-BILL-ih-kal) **cord** cord through which nourishment and oxygen flow from the mother to the baby during pregnancy; connected to the placenta and the baby's stomach

ultrasound (UL-tra-sound) **test** shows the development of a baby while inside the mother

urethra (you-REE-thra) tube through which urine passes out of the body; in the male this tube also carries semen

uterus (YOU-ter-us) pear-shaped organ that holds a growing baby; called womb in the Bible

vagina (va-JINE-ah) birth canal through which a baby passes to be born

vas deferens (VAS DEF-er-enz) tube that carries sperm from each testicle to a tube called the urethra

wet dream also called nocturnal emission (nok-TUR-nal e-MISH-un); release of excess semen during sleep

womb (woom) the word the Bible uses for uterus; the place where a baby grows until ready for birth

Answers to Questions

Answers to matching questions for "Carlee's Questions" on page 22:

1. d	7. c
2. f	8. i
3. h	9. a
4. j	10. k
5. b	11. g
6. e	

Answers to matching questions for "Rob and Dad Talk" on page 30:

1. h	6. d
2. f	7. g
3. e, i	8. b
4. c	9. j
5. a	

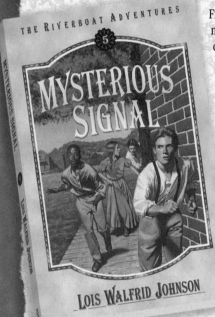

EXPLORE THE GREAT NORTHWOODS

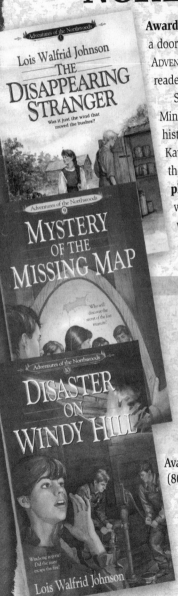

Award-winning author Lois Walfrid Johnson opens a door to another place and time with her bestselling ADVENTURES OF THE NORTHWOODS series for young readers.

Set in the early 1900s in northwest Wisconsin, Minnesota, and Michigan, these **compelling**, historically accurate stories introduce readers to Kate O'Connell, her stepbrother Anders, and their friend Erick Lundgren. The characters face **plenty of danger** and uncover lots of mysteries while learning **valuable lessons** about dealing with peer pressure, family relationships, and the need for unconditional love and forgiveness.

ADVENTURES OF THE NORTHWOODS

The Disappearing Stranger
The Hidden Message
The Creeping Shadows
The Vanishing Footprints
Trouble at Wild River
The Mysterious Hideaway
Grandpa's Stolen Treasure
The Runaway Clown
Mystery of the Missing Map
Disaster on Windy Hill

Available from your nearest Christian bookstore (800) 991-7747 or from Bethany House Publishers.

The Leader in Christian Fiction!
BETHANY HOUSE PUBLISHERS

11400 Hampshire Ave. South
Minneapolis, MN 55438

www.bethanyhouse.com